A Single
Headstrong
Heart

A Single Headstrong Heart

Kevin Myers

THE LILLIPUT PRESS
DUBLIN

First published 2016 by
THE LILLIPUT PRESS
62–63 Sitric Road, Arbour Hill
Dublin 7, Ireland
www.lilliputpress.ie

Copyright © Kevin Myers, 2016

ISBN 978 1 84351 4107

All rights reserved. No part of this publication may be reproduced in any form or by any means without the prior permission of the publisher.

A CIP record for this title is available from The British Library.

10 9 8 7 6 5 4 3 2 1

Set in 11.5 pt on 14.5 pt Garamond with Gotham display titling
Printed in Spain by Castuera

A Single
Headstrong
Heart

One

LOOK: you can find it yourself, on Google Earth: 17 Medina Road, Leicester, England. Observe the clutter of those three ugly angular roofs, and the flat one of the adjoining garage, upon which the three young Myerses once used to play. Of course, what you can't see is that there is no interior door from that garage to the kitchen just inches away – such a connection would have been logical, would it not? But there is little logic here in this house of the roofs, where almost nothing works quite as intended.

Thomas More coined the word Utopia, which literally means no place – a paradise where all is perfect. The imperial Victorians, confident there was something far worse than benign emptiness, accordingly concocted the term Dystopia, which essentially means 'a bad place'. Allow me to introduce you to my familial version of such locational quintessence: Myètopia, namely, a hive of patronymic ineptitude. And though you can gaze at the structural remains of Myètopia, now in flats, and may study its bizarre ugliness, you cannot see the secrets within those damp-brick, wind-scalded walls, or the tales that once unfolded beneath those unkempt, blue-slated roofs.

My first memory of this hive is of my lying alongside my twin sister Maggy, she a babbling little pupa in a woollen jumpsuit. I am on my favourite little mattress, from which I will not be parted. It reeks of the intimate persimmon fragrance of urine. My urine. Delicious. It is Christmas. My mother is one month away from giving birth to my baby brother Johnny. She is holding the ladder while Dad is attaching holly to a central point in the sitting-room ceiling, his throat rumbling with a curious combination of concentration and impatience that was to be as characteristic of him as a croak is to a bullfrog.

During the early months of 1939 when the Myers family was still very much a work in progress back in Ireland, Luftwaffe photo-reconnaissance aircraft secretly photographed every one of England's cities, and their aerial pictures of the western outskirts of Leicester clearly show the junction of Medina Road and Buckminster Road. There was no corner house there when Goering's men came a-calling, just vegetable allotments. But the owner of this blessed plot, a Jewish medical gentleman by the name of Dr Raussman, had already acquired a legally dubious planning permission to turn an angular section of that large cabbage patch into a site for a house, the construction of which was finished as darkness fell upon the world. Had Hitler, in his own characteristic way, not intervened, Leicester City Council might well in their own rather more municipal manner have obliged the developer to tear it down for his violation of the planning laws. But Adolf did intervene, it didn't, and so this tragic house survived.

However, the council planning officers wrought their revenge on Raussman (and thereby his hapless successor) by declaring that the road and entire pavement on the Buckminster Road side of this house, namely the surgery side, should indefinitely be declared 'unadopted'. In other words, it legally didn't exist: truly Myètopia. This meant that, by law, no public footpath or pavement or drainage or road gutters would or could be installed. Street sweepers would put their brooms on their shoulders and walk on by whenever they reached this house. Imagine: the only house in the entire area that was unpaved and undrained over its main frontage was the doctor's.

Nine years on my father bought this legally crippled property, and typically, without a proper document search. It was only after the family moved in that some of its shortcomings proclaimed themselves, the most obvious being the appearance of a muddy lake in front of the house for much of the year, which turned into a jungle of weeds, litter and dog shit in the summer. So Dad's patients had to traverse an assault course to get to and from him: that so many did was testament to the affection in which he was held. For Dad was a good doctor; a very good doctor indeed.

However, not content with this grievous outside infirmity, 17 Medina Road was also maimed internally. Each bedroom had a fatuous bell-push connected to a bell-board in the kitchen, which identified the chamber that required the attention of the scullery maid, though of course she had joined the Baltic states in a common extinction the same year as the house was completed. These bedrooms formed most of the upper floor of a half-cruciform structure that had two small wings on a central core. Each wing consisted of a single bedroom with three outside, uninsulated and bitterly cold walls. Every single window frame in the house seems to have been made from a special 1939 pig iron that had rapidly rusted and warped soon after installation, thereby generously allowing endless gales to share our living space.

This was the house that my parents moved into soon after the twins' birth. Three siblings had already pioneered the first half of the Myers family – The Big Ones, as they came to be called, Ann, Bill and David, over a period of four years in Ireland – and then The Little Ones in Leicester, firstly Maggy and me, six years after David, and finally, three years after us, came Johnny. The Three Little Ones inhabited an astonishingly evil bedroom whose primary purpose seems to have been to toughen us up for an adulthood in a Siberian gulag. Even in summer, the inside of the three walls exposed to the elements had the icy caress of an igloo: in winter, the entire room felt as if no one had even built the igloo. At least the northern wall lacked a window, thus sparing us the benedictions of the Arctic. The one facing eastward showed no such mercy, for it contained a triple-window through whose ill-fitting frames whistled all the winds that the North Sea could generate. They arrived like assassins that had casually knifed people to death on the Cambridgeshire fenlands, before hurrying onwards to their real business in our bedroom. The adjoining south-facing wall could and should have had a window, but of course didn't, thus sparing us the demoralizing light and feminizing warmth of the noonday sun.

A single wall connected this bedroom with the rest of the house along a brief corridor. The first door to the left in this corridor led to the lavatory, a bitterly freezing cubicle with another east-facing window, the warped iron edges of which provided all the natural ventilation you could possibly want. Not even the sturdiest of Emperor Penguins could linger for long over its rectal duties here. Next to this was the bathroom, with a heat-extracting linoleum floor that instantly rewarded our usually slipper-less feet with bone-deep chilblains. The morning ritual of brushing our teeth was done flamingo-like, perched on one foot, to minimize frostbite on the other. Steam had so warped and rusted the window frame here that only an adult could force it shut. But even then, naturally, it welcomed all Arctic gales, in this, the room where we were most often naked – oh but not for long.

Next came the warmest and only south-facing bedroom in the house, generally used by my big sister Ann. Ahead, at the end of this little passageway, in a calamitous mirror-image of the first room, lay my parents' bedroom. It too could have had a south-facing and warming window, but naturally didn't. A little corridor opposite Ann's bedroom led first to an abominably dark bedroom on the right, used by Bill and David, and beyond that, the stairs to the ground floor.

Most of main wall of the kitchen wall downstairs was taken up with a huge range constructed on very Myersian principles, namely, how to burn vast amounts of fuel without generating any energy whatsoever. It was like some Aztec god, full of wrath and spleen, being used but once in my memory, and after it filled the kitchen with vast clouds of soot and Andean quantities of cold, no one was ever impertinent enough to intrude upon its iron slumbers again. Henceforth, it served as a large mouse sanctuary, whose wizened, frostbitten citizenry would occasionally totter out over the ice-cold stone floor, vainly looking for warmth. In the corner of the kitchen was also a gas-powered boiler for laundry, and which stank of old soap powder and what I now recognize as the strangely semen-like reek of crusted suds.

The kitchen opened onto a gloomy and unheated hall that was the interface between the Myers family and the outside world. Here lay the inner door to the surgery and to those whooping, wheezing, seeping things, patients. Dad's examining room came first and beyond it the waiting room. This contained a few chairs, an ashtray, naturally, for the more fastidious of Dad's patients, and a few fantastically old women's magazines that seemed to have predated colour printing. The far door opened onto Buckminster Road, and the malarial swamps beyond.

Let us return now to the inner hall, which also had a north-facing glass front door leading to Medina Road. (Only a Myers house would have had a glass door gazing at the Arctic). Two other doors from the hall led respectively to a small dining-room and the drawing-room, the latter, like my bedroom, having three exposed walls for exporting warmth to the open air. One wall contained a generous concession to sizzling 1939-style modernity, a recess to hold a large wireless. For the first six years of my life, this recess was to provide the household with an aural window to the outside world. It was the only window in the entire house without draughts.

The Myers family were Catholic, intensely so. From infancy, Maggy and I had a little shrine with candles and statues of Jesus and Mary in our bedroom, and a little bacterial font of holy water on the wall beside the door in which we would routinely bless ourselves, a regular germ-swap that left us with stinking fingers. Uranium-rich luminous statues glowed on our bedside tables, bombarding us with gene-mutating radioactive alpha particles through our grace-filled slumbers. Maybe it was our piety alone that prevented us from sprouting antlers and dorsal fins or dying of font-borne infections. And certainly in my case, there was actually little difference in my childish mind between Irishness and Catholicism.

This world view coloured our local vision also – and let me here dispose of the standard myths about a heartless England being bigoted against Irish immigrants. Well, possibly in earlier years, but certainly not in my own experience. Leicester folk accepted strangers in their midst without complaint or even curiosity, though the then entirely new name 'Kevin' induced a rhapsody of incomprehension amongst the locals, for it seemed as full of consonants as a rare Polish place-name. Indeed, if there was any prejudice, it was ours, for we Myerses tended to pity our poor Protestant neighbours for their indolent godlessness. While they lay abed on Sunday mornings our family would be gone from dawn's early light to form the congregational centre of gravity in the heart of St Peter's Church a couple of miles from our home. We usually walked while my father slept on – notionally, that there would always be someone in the house in an emergency. But I think the real reason was that he liked the peace of a child-free household, for we Myers children, Big and Little Ones alike, were noisy. We brawled. A lot.

The first neighbours Maggy and I got to know were the Thompsons, whose house formed the bottom boundary of our back garden. They were, I suppose, quite ancient – in their late forties, at least. Mr Thom moved, acted and thought like a roadkill mole breathing its last. Most of the adult men in my childhood had served in the war, but not even Britain's darkest hour could have merited a military deployment for this living embodiment of perpetual somnolence. Wordless docility, interrupted by long periods of sleep, were the bipolar extremes between which he was torn. Mr Thom would spend the entire day in his armchair slowly smoking his pipe, each puff requiring vast amounts of measured thought. Otherwise, he passed his hours in sleep, from some of which he emerged each morning to drive to work a mile away, blinking in astonishment at his own temerity. My imagination is neither rich nor impoverished enough to envisage an employer who could possibly have found a use for him, other than as a shop-window dummy in an armchair. As for Mr Thom and sex, one may as well speculate about the libido of suet.

Mrs Thom was the complete opposite to her husband, a bundle of tireless energy, bathed with sweat from the physical exertions with which she filled her day as she scrubbed and wiped and polished and washed and dug and peeled and cut. She also sometimes indulged some strange tastes: my family, almost obsessively, closed and triple-locked the lavatory door. Mrs Thom, however, would take me into the downstairs toilet with her, and make me stand right beside her while, with many squints, grunts and sighs, she attended to her various businesses, which might take some time. Age has suggested this business might have consisted of more than I knew of then. She absolutely did not abuse me.

Occasionally, in the summer, the Thoms would take Maggy and me to the seaside resort of Skegness. The journey for most people in those days from Leicester, along the eighty miles of old stagecoach roads through the market towns of Rutland and Lincolnshire, was about three hours. Mr Thom did it in roughly three days. We would leave at dawn and get home upon some subsequent midnight, having spent a few minutes eating candyfloss on the cold black mire that served as a beach where the North Sea washed the sullen shores of England. Mrs Thom would usually improvise a shack of deckchairs, behind which we sheltered from the unremitting Siberian gale. If this ever abated, she might accompany Maggie and me a-paddling, while beneath his little black trilby Mr Thom fell headlong into his usual coma. After wading halfway to Scandinavia, we three Argonauts would still be only up to our ankles in the icy grey pond that is the North Sea in high summer. We would gaze at distant Norway for a while, and austerely Norway would gaze back at us, before we forded the cold wide shallows back to shore. There we would wake Mr Thom who would return us pell-mell to Leicester in his ancient Morris, never leaving second gear, his hat perched on his head and his pipe obliquely in his mouth, while he lay back in his seat and comprehensively proved the viability of sleep-driving. The moment we got back to Medina Road, no matter the hour, poor Mrs Thom would start cleaning floors and polishing garden spades and laying bricks and sweeping chimneys, or even shooing me into the lavatory for some of those strange squinty moments of hers.

Yes, for us Myerses it was always lavatory, at my mother's class-conscious insistence, for even beneath the bizarre assembly of roofs and rooms that was our home she had an acute sense of social status. Hence L-A-V-A-T-O-R-Y, never toilet. In which regard, Dad was a more attentive parent than were most men of his generation, though I deeply distrusted his ablutionary techniques. Personal hygiene was achieved in those days with Jeyes toilet paper, which neither was made of paper, nor for use in a toilet. It did not clean, or absorb or remove, but simply redistributed whatever it found. I suspect that Jeyes' real manufacturing skill lay in the making of war-time butter knives, which could spread a little margarine a very long way indeed. That said, my mother's deft toiling nonetheless generally left my bottom feeling as it had been reasonably cleansed; however, Dad's efforts would usually leave me feeling as he had been spreading warm jam.

Dad was also responsible for the garden. Accordingly, in our north-facing flowerbed, which was totally shaded from the sun by a high fence, lay our rose garden. Opposite, receiving the warm benedictions of a southern sun, prospered a nondescript and largely accidental assembly of plant life, which included docks, dandelions and other weeds, and – by some miraculous accident – a colony of hollyhocks. Now I firmly believed that if you treated a bee with kindness, then in return she would do you no harm. So I regularly captured bees in the hollyhock blossoms, holding them gently between finger and thumb and stroking them. I was never stung, thereby vindicating my theory that if you mean no ill to anyone, then no ill will be done to you. Of all of childhood's lessons, that surely had to be the most fatuous.

At the age of four, Maggy and I went were sent to the strangely named Hazeldean High School for Infants, run by an elderly Mrs Ball and her portly daughter Miss Ball. Apart from the very first time, when Dad drove us, Maggy and I walked there and back every day, a journey of two miles, through several major traffic junctions. Not even the delusions of memory can conceal the meteorological truth that it rained an awful lot in those days, and we often arrived at school soaking wet. The children's overcoats were all dried next to the coke-burning stove that heated the classroom, and the smell of wet wool and sodden gabardine remains as evocative for me as any madeleine. Since little boys in those days really did not even know how to walk, I would run homeward through the leaves shed by the trees along Fosse Park, kicking them into little tumults of indignation. My poor sister, with her satchel flapping on her hip, tottered way behind me.

'I runned and I runned, and I pulled up my socks, and I runned and I runned, and I pulled up my socks, but I still couldn't catched him,' lamented Maggy in the freezing yet steaming kitchen of Medina Road.

That November we celebrated Guy Fawkes' Night with fireworks in the back garden. Next morning I was unwell and Maggy, aged five, walked off to school alone. Wandering outside from my sickbed in my pyjamas, I found some huge bangers, which Dad had – naturally – failed to put away. Holding them in my hands, I lit them one by one and watched them explode. In those days, when it took a lot to impress Guy Fawkes revellers who were veterans of El Alamein and Monte Casino, bangers were like baby grenades, and these regularly cost incautious adults their hands and eyes. My tiny fingers escaped each blast, though my hair and face were rather scorched. Mum came out and found me as the last banger exploded in my still amazingly intact hand.

By this time I had also discovered true love, in the shape of the deputy head of Hazeldean, Miss Ball. That she was at least seven times both my age and weight was no impediment to an intrepid banger-holder like me so, naturally, I told her that I intended to marry her, and at the very first opportunity. With solumn gravity, she accepted my offer. However, we men can be a capricious species, and I'm sorry to say that my eyes were soon diverted by Sheila, the girl with whom I shared a desk.

She, you see, had taken pity on my hopelessly boyish illiteracy, and would carefully correct my misshapen letters: thus was my heart quite smitten by her beauty, her curls, her crayons. But it didn't take long for my rampant inconstancy to reveal itself yet again, after she had rather spectacularly crapped herself, just inches from where I sat, skilfully adjusting her knickers so that their contents were deposited on the bench seat beside me. It is an unusual fellow that can overlook such largesse, and alas, I was not that man.

My turmoil-filled sex life took a turn for the exotic next with a pretty young teacher called Miss Clark, my attraction for whom depended more on anatomical curiosity than unmixed Platonic love. One afternoon in the playground, a ball bounced up her dress, but apparently did not re-emerge, despite her frantic jumping up and down. Love can be fuelled by many things: on this occasion – and not for the first time in the deplorable history of the male sex – it was curiosity about what was going on under her skirts. I am moreover, to be forgiven for my devotion, for

Miss Clark – the vixen! – also trailed the heady fragrance of exotic scents. I rest my case.

Away from the temptress-filled seraglio that was Hazeldean High School, Nonie Parker was another woman who took my fancy, though in a rather more substantive way. I knew that she and her husband Michael were very different from us Myerses, but of course I didn't really know why or how. They were in fact the quintessence of middle-class Englishness, being decent, sweet, awkward, kind, honourable and true. They spoke in a strange dialect, one which had expired over most of England, save in the remoter corners of continuity on the BBC Home Service, with the mannered tones of Sylvia Peters or Mary Malcolm, and in royal broadcasts from Buckingham Palace. It is the voice one only hears today in reshowings of *Brief Encounter*. Michael had briefly worked with Dad soon after qualifying as a doctor, and remaining a regular visitor thereafter. For some reason he always arrived with what he called cream cakes, though they were actually composed of wallpaper adhesive, cellophane and granulated glass, and would have been absolutely ideal for blocking up Medina Road's windows. Michael would gaze raptly as we laboured grimly through his Stalingrad of confectionery, and Nonie (as gaunt and elegant as Mrs Simpson, though unlike that royal raptor, radiating a very special kindness) would occasionally bathe us with the sweetest of smiles.

Nonie was regal, while skinny Michael, in his ill-fitting three-piece suits and baggy trousers, was jolly and kind and awkwardly boyish. He was also a shrewd doctor. I had a chronic cough, which had resisted antibiotics and all emollients. Finally Michael insisted he be allowed to examine me, and his eyes narrowed just inches away from mine.

'Got you, you rascal!' he cried, sticking a forceps down my throat. A moment later, out came a length of straw that had been stuck, almost invisibly, in the soft tissue of the uvula. Cough cured. But that wasn't the reason why I liked the Parkers, and particularly liked sitting on Nonie's lap. I now realize that I could detect from her the pheromones of raw sexuality. No wonder Michael Parker was always smiling.

We had two daily helps, Mrs Shaw and Mrs Lett. The former was an utterly unservile servant who was always threatening me with the strangely Freudian injunction, 'You watch yourself, or I'll cut your tail off.' Mrs Lett was the opposite, a reassuringly benign domestic who insisted on working for free, because, apparently, Dad had saved her husband's life.

Mrs Lett and Mrs Shaw worked on different days, but both turned up on Mondays for the Operation Overlord that was the weekly laundry – a brutal ritual that the rotary washing machine has made as obsolete as human sacrifice. The burden of cleanliness was in those days truly unspeakable, and its vassalage remains – for all the communications miracles – the greatest difference between those times and today. It was borne entirely by women. The Myers wash was done in the great big gas-powered boiler. The entire kitchen was turned into a Turkish bath during this vast amphibious operation, and the women became puce-faced myrmidons of sweat as they uncoiled snakes of wet linen from the innards of the cauldron and slowly fed them through the hand-cranked wringer. Wet laundry was hung on an overhead clothes rack if it was raining, but usually, no matter how grey the day, the outside clothes line would be put to work. My mother's entire peace of mind for the week was completely dominated by that Monday wash and the weather's designs upon it.

I associate no particular memory smell with my mother, whereas Dad reeked of cigarettes, the subtle odours of manliness, and of shaving foam. Standing before the draught-caressed bathroom sink in his vest, he lathered himself each morning with a badger-hair brush and a stick of soap, and unleashed the thin Gillette safety razor, the blades for which came in packets of five in small blue-green cardboard packets. Each blade was apparently wrapped in the kind of greaseproof paper that had been used by Jeyes to make their lavatory paper, and it seemed almost impossible to open without severing an artery. The rituals of the morning shave were quite fascinating: the smell of oily lather, the hot water from the little tap (marked '1939') instantly turning cold in the frozen basin, the doomed steam being wafted away by the hearty gale through the window frames, and the sense of imminent bloodshed.

Another of the rhythms of our childhood was provided by the regular arrival of the coal lorry, manned by sinewy, coughing tar-devils with leather aprons, padded shoulders and white eyes wildly staring from blackened faces. The coal varied dramatically in quality, some burning with the gusto of wet pumice, reducing the mean temperature of Medina Road to slightly above that of Greenland. One winter Dad put in an order for logs. Naturally, our coal supplies ran out before the logs had arrived, and equally naturally, one afternoon, with the temperatures dropping, it began to snow.

Dad gazed outside and said: 'What about it, young fellow me lad? What about you and me going up to Bradgate Park?' I was ecstastic. Me and him! Alone! Brilliant.

'Bradgate Park? But Billy, it's far too cold for him,' protested Mum.

'He'll be fine, won't you, young fellow me lad?'

I certainly would. If my dad was going to walk in Bradgate Park, I was going to go with him, no matter how cold. We drove the eight miles there, me in a velvet overcoat, short trousers, knee-length socks, mittens and little shoes. We began walking through the deserted parklands, past the ruins of the house of the child-usurper Lady Jane Grey, she who had been queen for a week, before Queen Mary deposed her and skilfully restored her own Tudor bottom to the throne of England, while removing poor Jane's head from her Grey shoulders. On the high hill beyond the brickwork rubble of the ruined house lay Old John, a stone folly of great mystery to all the children of Leicestershire. We believed that there were secret passageways from the folly to the centre of Leicester, to Buckingham Palace, to anywhere.

Deer gazed at us. The cold was astonishing, and bit right into my shin bones. My feet were no more. Halfway up the hill, Dad asked: 'Do want to go back? We can pretend we went all the way.'

'No fear,' I replied stoutly.

'By Jove! You're a plucky one,' he chuckled admiringly.

I was so proud of his pride that I would happily have walked all the way to the Arctic, in my thin shoes, my socks with garters below the knee and my baggy grey flannel shorts. We trudged through the virgin shin-deep snow, right up to the top of Old John, and there stood beside the great stone folly, father and son, hand in frozen hand, gazing over a great iceland that was utterly uninhabited but for us and the curious deer.

My bone marrow burned like steel rods as we walked back to the car, which, lacking any heater, brought no relief, while the skin of my thighs stuck onto the frozen leather of the seat. At home, we found that the delivery man had dumped the logs onto the driveway, blocking the garage. They would have to be moved. Dad told me to go in and he would attend to it, but I refused, and so between us we carried the logs to the side of the house. I was torn between the pride of doing something usefully adult and the exquisite agony of carrying these frozen, resinous logs, one by one, in my little mittened hands, the fingers of which I seemed determined to lose, through either explosives or exposure. My older brothers, David and Bill, emerged from the modest penumbra of semi-warmth that still lingered in the kitchen, like an Indian tribe expelled from its icefield and facing extinction, in order to give a hand, but in my eyes the glory was mine, the day was mine and Dad was mine.

The logs turned out to be green, and once (by dint of some fairly violent firelighting) they were finally burning they behaved like heat-absorbing igneous sponges, hissing sullenly and dripping sweet-smelling pools of gum onto the hearth. We reverted to coal thereafter.

MAGGY WAS quicker than me at everything and had a surer grasp of the outside world. Speaking of a neighbour, Mum said to Dad one afternoon at teatime: 'Mrs Padstow's in labour.'

'What does in labour mean?' I asked.

'It means she supports Mr Atlee,' pronounced Maggy sagely.

'King George is dead,' my mother said one day before our morning prayers in the sitting room. 'We must now pray for his soul.'

'Who's King George?' I asked Maggy, who generally knew things.

'He's the king,' she said.

'Ah,' I said, satisfied.

At school, Mrs Ball walked into the class in tears. 'King George is dead,' she announced. 'Class will stand for a minute in silence.' Weeping, she left.

'Why's Mrs Ball roaring?' asked Sheila, my former inamorata ('roaring' in Leicester means to weep emotionally).

'The king is dead,' I explained.

'Búgger me, I thought she meant her blúddy dog were dead,' opined Edward Warwick, the bad boy of the class.

Mrs Padstow certainly didn't support Mr Atlee, the leader of the Labour Party. Nobody in our part of Leicester (most of them barely a generation away from being working class) would have voted anything other than Conservative. Indeed, an irrational loathing of the Labour Party formed a profoundly important part of the neighbourhood culture. This was no doubt due to many things – class insecurity, tribal solidarity, upwardly mobile ambition, but most powerfully of all, snobbery. I soaked in this deplorable culture, and from an early age, was fluent in the nuances of class, effortlessly able to distinguish between the various social strata of Leicester and their many accents, above all which rested – in my view – the Myers family. Our largely RP accents were what mostly distinguished us. Leicester folk speak a variety of Danelaw English that is quite rustic, and pleasing to the ear: aside from its 'aints', for which Mum would have slain us, its 'u' sound rhymes with the 'oo' of book, and is rendered in these pages as ú.

It was also a sorry truth that the more working class the accent, the tougher the customer; and none tougher at Hazeldean than Edward Warwick.

Children ate lunch in the school, and though the main courses were not too offensive, desserts were usually catastrophic. Even now, the very words 'tapioca' and 'semolina' ring in my ears like medieval curses.

One day Edward Warwick refused to eat his pudding of uncooked frogspawn. Miss Clark reported this to Mrs Ball, who arrived in the dining hall like an executioner, and standing right behind Edward, told him in the most terrifying tones that he wouldn't be allowed to go home, EVER, until he'd finished it. If she'd spoken to me like that I'd have eaten my feet. Confident of her victory, she walked away from Edward, and as she reached the door, he bawled at the top of his voice: 'Eh úp, you big fat fúckin' cow, ah'm gonna tell me Mam on you, and she's gonna cúm rahn' 'ere and pull down your fúckin' knickers and spank your bare búm till you're fúckin' roarin'.'

The resulting silence could have reached out and stopped the traffic in New York. How long it lasted, I could not say. A week maybe? Then the wrath of Mrs Ball fell upon poor Edward Warwick, and he was swept from the dining-room and from the school, vanishing from it for ever.

But enough of the sex and violence of Hazeldean High School for Infants. Allow me to introduce you to the dramatis personae of Medina Road. Across the way from the Myers lived the Pattersons: Mr and Mrs, he a boorish, bald and sneering snooker-hall manager, she motherly and fat, whose barrage-balloon pantaloons festooned the Patterson clothes line. No image from my childhood quite matches the enduring potency of Mrs Patterson's knickers flapping in the breeze. The Pattersons had three boys: their surly teenage sons, John and Jim, and their youngest boy, Mark, who was my age and my friend.

Next to them were the Whites, a slight social layer beneath the Pattersons, and of whom I knew little. Mr Smith, bald and moustached, was a mechanic of some kind. Ann Smith was the same age as us, a wild, scrawny, fascinating hillbilly, but alas, she didn't play with us. I never knew why; possibly the inscrutable chemistry of class. She had a brother, Graham, who spent his entire life wrestling with spanners under a car, from which he would occasionally emerge, usually the week before Christmas, an oil-covered replica of a coalman.

Next to the Whites lived the Padstows: Mrs Padstow, a vast, cheerful woman, her husband Dick, a true yeoman of England, decent, honest and true, and one of the finest man I ever met, and two girls, Susan, about the same age as us, plus baby Patricia. Next to them were the Frosts, an elderly couple who were sweet and invisible, and whom death could scarcely make more inconspicuous, and, as we were one day to discover, really didn't.

Alongside us were the Thompsons, and next to them were the Heddicks, who were a gallant attempt by Medina Road to show that England could produce a family as chaotic and noisy as the Myerses, but far, far poorer and dirtier. It was said that they had won a little money on the football pools, so enabling them to buy their modest terraced house. Like most of our neighbours they couldn't pronounce the letter 'h', so they said they were 'Eddicks. Their son Keith once invited us to a birthday party. A jelly was presented. Quivering inside it was a dead mouse. The robust Heddicks ate round the corpse, and none too squeamishly, while we gaping Myerses watched with frozen spoons.

One afternoon Maggy and I returned home to find all our neighbours standing on their doorsteps and gazing raptly at some workmen on our roof. Cars had stopped on the street, and passers-by gathered in small entranced clusters, staring upwards. This was probably Medina Road's most enthralling event since the Luftwaffe had visited. A trembling Mr Padstow called me over, his eyes never leaving the entrancing sight over my shoulder.

'Ey úp, Kev. Is tha' wha' ah think i' is? A real television aerial?' he asked, in the tones of such wonderment as an interplanetary space station might have merited.

'Yes,' declared Little Lord Fauntleroy haughtily.

'Oo ya beauty,' he replied, which is the standard Leicester exclamation for anything that defies further comment.

The new TV had a screen the size of a small paperback book on a walnut console that was as large as the washing machine that we did not yet have. The term 'black and white' is still used about those television sets, though they were utterly incapable of conveying either extreme, settling for barely distinguishable shades of grey. Nonetheless, the television seemed impossibly exotic, and I would occasionally, and with much noblesse oblige, invite Mark and Susan to come and enjoy some small portions of it. And small they were, for the BBC only broadcast programmes rather like a works canteen served meals.

However, I simply don't know whether the television had been ordered specifically for us to watch the coronation of Queen Elizabeth, which was the great public event of my childhood. That summer of 1953 the streets of a dreary English midland town suddenly became brilliantly colourful as they sprouted thousands of union jacks. In the working-class terraces a few hundred yards away from the Myers home, all the housewives, their hair tied with knotted headscarves over their scalps, spent the day before the coronation on their knees, hand-scrubbing their front steps and the entire pavements with carbolic soap in parallel strips of loyal cleanliness. Above them fluttered a panoply of red white and blue pennants.

The Myers house filled with guests to watch the flickering grey images of the coronation, the sitting room as densely packed as a football terrace. Mum had laid on the largest feast we had ever seen, complete with sandwiches, sausage rolls and cake, sherry, whiskey and Guinness to toast the young queen's health. When she had been crowned, and the national anthem began, Dad rose, and led us all, Irish and English, in a fervid rendition of 'God Save the Queen'.

That evening I ran across the road to share my excitement with the Padstows. I found Mrs Padstow feeding her latest child, Patricia, with a bosom the size of a small English county. She offered me some celebratory dolly mixtures, as she unhibitedly unholstered her unemployed breast and shifted the baby to it, leaving both breasts exposed. I gazed on in happy awe, for I was absolutely certain that, equipped with superbly monstrous mammaries like these, verily creations of God Himself, she must surely be responsible for feeding all the children of Leicester.

The coronation of Queen Elizabeth II, Defender of the Faith, Monarch of the United Kingdom of Great Britain and Northern Ireland, Head of the Commonwealth of Nations, means many things to people who lived through that time. To me, the public memory is of Dad leading us in loyal celebration of the young queen; the more private one is of a boundless supply of sweets and a wondrous amplitude of Padstow bosom.

Two

IRELAND. It hovered like an El Dorado in our childhood imaginations. On Saturday mornings my father would lie in bed, singing the songs of his childhood with the strong melodious baritone with which he had once distantly serenaded the new queen. This was how I first heard 'The Kerry Dances', 'The Rose of Tralee' and 'The Minstrel Boy', as his voice carried downstairs, and Mum was making the breakfast. I knew from early experience that Ireland was inhabited by kindly, colourful, vibrant and musical people, who went to Mass in happy droves on Sundays, owned donkeys, and ate delicious Haffner's sausages with white pudding at every single meal, which made it about as perfect a place as ever a place could be.

Ireland was, moreover, possessed of another bounty, for between them the Myerses and my mother's family, the Teevans, had produced an army of uncles and aunts of an almost Dickensian goodness. Our annual holiday in the ancestral homeland was like a visit to the benigner regions of *David Copperfield*, with some fresh Peggoty and Barkus at every turn. Moreover, there were many Teevan cousins, who were tumultuous, chaotic, anarchic, gregarious and unguarded. These pilgrimages to Ireland lasted a month, in the Delgany and Greystones areas of County Wicklow. The villages of Leicestershire were manicured, neat and orderly, and peopled by the decent but rather reticent and mannered folk of middle England. The villages of Wicklow were splattered with cow dung and populated by cheery men in old caps sitting on walls, who talked to complete strangers at noon. Milk in Leicestershire magically came in bottles marked Kirby & West. In Wicklow, grinning donkeys bore warm churns of it to collection points. Irish children never wore socks or had proper haircuts or shorts that fitted, and they seemed so entirely spontaneous compared to their polite, neat equivalents in Leicester, Edward Warwick notwithstanding.

The ferry to Dun Laoghaire always arrived as the evening Angelus sounded across the bay, and the more pious of the homeward-bound travellers would exultantly proclaim its words over the butting swell, 'The angel of the Lord, declared unto Mary ...'

One year we were staying in a small Dun Laoghaire hotel for a couple of days because our Greystones house wasn't yet vacant. We Myers children were shouting so much that the manager came to our room and told us to be quiet. I was so proud. We could outshout the Irish; how brilliant was that? I loved Ireland. It had large American cars, and green buses, and really exotic coins, and it had the wild, blue-coloured, heather-covered hills of Wicklow, wherein babbled the deep-set trout streams that simply did not exist in the canalized river valleys of Leicestershire.

My father seemed to feel exile most keenly in the absence of these, and also Haffner's sausages. In preparation for our annual return to Wicklow, he would pass many hours in his little workshop at home, making dry-flies that were all glittering solder, evil barb and flashing feather. We Myerses would spend most of our Irish holidays on Greystones beach, while Dad would often depart to do some angling with his rods and his velvet-cushioned metal case of dry flies. Sometimes I would go with him and lie on the riverbank, while he, standing in his thigh-high waders, would cast for hour after hour, and for all his energy and patience, catching almost nothing. How could he do otherwise? His heavy, home-made flies would hit the water's surface like small mortar bombs. This was not so much angling as an artillery shoot. The only possible way for him to catch a trout at all would be for a projectile to break its skull with a direct hit.

After the futile angling would come the fry-up, and invariably with a Primus stove that in moral squalor absolutely matched 17 Medina Road. Since no one knows (and with good reason) what a Primus stove is any more, I'll describe it: its base consisted of a paraffin tank, which contained a small hand pump for putting the fuel under pressure. Above the tank was a little metal gas ring containing a central bath, in which methylated spirits would be burning. As the paraffin gas emerged, it would be ignited by the burning meths, and thereafter, the paraffin gas, provided it was constantly repumped, would provide a pure blue, self-sustaining flame.

This does not even begin to convey the sordid reality of how a Primus stove behaved in real life, which was as follows: after an afternoon spent hurling dry flies into gently idling streams, where they would explode like small grenades, causing all fish to scatter like schoolgirls from a flasher, Dad would take out the Primus, the pan, the sausages, the kettle. Because the stove had spindly little legs, it would usually fall over when pumped, scattering the meths. For reasons that cannot possibly be explained, the top of the tank had a small blade attached, which could be relied on to slice into the nearest available finger. Even with me holding the base steady at arm's length, my face buried into the Wicklow loam, and Dad pumping frantically, the paraffin gas would usually choose not to be ignited, and then the meths would burn out. So we'd have to start again. Fresh meths into the ring, fresh pumping by Dad, then he'd hurriedly fumble with his spare hand to strike a match to light the meths – except, of course, he hasn't got a spare hand, because one hand is pumping, the other is holding the match, but nothing is holding the striking surface of the matchbox. At which point I would knock over the stove, spilling the last of the meths, or Dad would impale his thumb on the blade, and then try to choke or kick the Primus to death.

And finally, homeward, Haffnerless and hungry.

One day lives with me with perfect clarity down the decades. The entire family had joined Dad in the Myers car – Standard Vanguard KBC 100 – on his futile angling-and-Primus expedition, and after a sandwich picnic (Mum was no fool) we drove back towards Greystones through the heather-mauve, bright-green, slate-grey Wicklow hills. The BBC Light Programme was on the car radio, and we heard that England had just reclaimed the Ashes for the first time in twenty years. We all cheered, and as we did, Petula Clark followed, with 'The Shoemaker'. It was 19 August 1953, and I was six years old.

The rest of that holiday we Myerses sat on the beach and gazed eastwards towards Wales, occasionally immersing our bony white bodies in the nicely chilled waters that heaved and lapped onto the grey pebbles of the well-named Greystones. My father and my uncle, his brother-in-law the stonemason Martin Coffey, round and bald and with a handkerchief on his pink scalp, would gaze at fish leaping (probably trying to escape the freezing sea) and murmuring the things that men say when their sandalled feet are as cold as the very gravestones on which Martin made his living.

An interest in women's bodies, which had been initially piqued by Mrs Padstow's (entirely innocent) display of breast, and then enhanced by the mystery of the vanishing ball up Miss Clark's skirt, was further whetted when a well-known madwoman began to undress completely on the beach, the final nudity of which I was denied sight of by Mum throwing a towel over my avidly gazing face.

But alas, Mum's protective reflexes turned to stone with the arrival of her thoroughly clothed sister, the Gorgon, Aunt Enid Orr, as malignant as that first Romanov daemon who chose to make haemophilia her legacy. My father hated Enid. Though Irish-born, she always spoke of herself as British, to the teeth-grinding frustration of her brothers, my uncles Tom, Jim and Harry, who were passionately, desperately, overwhelmingly proud of their Irishness. Moreover, Enid was a cruel woman. Neither my father, a man who was usually resistant to the commands of the human hierarchy, nor my mother, almost a generation younger than her sister, could resist the galleon majesty of her willpower.

For two years running she came to Greystones to take Maggy and Johnny on a day trip to Dublin, while rigorously excluding me.

'You are a horrid little boy, and to show you how horrid you are, I'm leaving you here,' she would declare through her huge lipstick-covered false teeth, before departing with my siblings in tow. They would return at the end of the day, laden with goodies, which munificence was intended to provoke jealousy in my young heart. But that stranger to love did not know – how could she? – that I relished her visitations, because they meant that I had Mum and Dad to myself, while poor Maggy and Johnny had to endure *her*.

One reason why Dad let her get away with her capers was her social status. William Myers was born of far humbler stock. His father had been a policeman, but Dad and his two sisters, Nell and Patty, were raised by his uncle Jack Myers, a fireman, and Uncle Jack's spinster sister Margaret. A third sister, Maureen, died of TB, which could almost an acronym for 'taboo', and so was never mentioned. (The family grave in Glasnevin Cemetery in Dublin even today remains an essay in lapidary reticence: it is simply marked Myers.)

Dad was educated by the Christian Brothers at Synge Street in Dublin, where they beat him every day, perhaps to convey some generalized and not entirely inaccurate lesson that life is unfair. He hated the school, yet later became a teacher's assistant there: of a law-abiding, compliant nature, clearly. And by some improbable alchemy, this working-class boy, in days when working-class boys invariably remained working-class boys, was able to magic a place as student at the Royal College of Surgeons of Ireland. This rather bespeaks a powerful sense of purpose.

As a young medical graduate, my father befriended a Harry Teevan, a doctor's son who was blessed as a teller of hysterically funny stories. In comparison, poor Dad must have seemed somewhat dull – decent and upright, the policeman's son, raised in a law-abiding, loyal and uniformed household.

Through Harry, Dad met my mother, Norah. She had spent her childhood in a grubby little Irish hamlet called Hackballscross, which paradoxically had once been known as Myers's Cross. During the Troubles in 1919–21, when she was a child, British forces or the IRA, fresh from the squalid little ambushes that seem to characterize most Irish wars, would hammer on the front door, looking for Dr Francis Teevan to come out and treat their wounded.

My mother's family was large: Enid, Tom, Jim, Harry, Norah and Kevin, plus her sister poor Maureen, who – with what turned out to be a deplorably nominative kismet – also died of TB in her teens. A transfer to Dublin followed, where Dr Teevan practised medicine and lectured at the Royal College of Surgeons. Mum's family lived in a rather grand house in Sunbury Gardens, complete with servants. For some reason, she was sent away to school at the Loreto Convent in St Alban's, where she acquired a very English accent.

My father was about thirty-four and she twenty-four when they met. He was a handsome young man, with a strong jaw and cheekbones and deep penetrating eyes. His private life (this is the non-prurient way of saying 'sex life') during his twenties and early thirties remains an utter mystery to me. Norah Teevan was small and slight, a pretty girl, with high cheekbones and a fine slim nose. Her hair was jet black and her eyes a clear blue. I am not inclined to speculate about her private life. She and Dad were wed in June 1936, not in Dublin, but rather oddly, and rather modestly, in the ferry port of Dun Laoghaire, where neither lived, whence they instantly hurried to London and their honeymoon.

The old unionist, Protestant ruling class had been leaving this aggressively Catholic Ireland in their many thousands after independence in 1922, and I know my mother, who was deeply class conscious, would have preferred to live in the socially salubrious (and once largely Protestant) suburbs on the southside. Instead, my parents found themselves in a new house in Mobhi Road, Glasnevin, on the northside of Dublin. It was ugly, but its location suited Dad, for he had found a job as the northside doctor to the Dublin Tramways & Bus Company: a secure job, come hell or high water.

Children followed. Ann in 1937, William in 1939, David in 1941. War had broken out just over two months after William's birth, and Ireland – without an army, navy, air force or treaty obligation to do otherwise – had opted for a prudential neutrality. But the country had already distanced itself from all other lands, in an economically and socially ruinous experiment in moral isolationism: so it was now perforce, if rather fortunately, excluded from the greater events that were to shape the rest of mankind. However, 100,000 Irishmen and women chose to make Hitler's business their business, and one of these was Norah's young brother Kevin, a doctor.

I like what I see of Kevin Teevan. We have photographs of him, mud-besplattered on the rugby pitch, hurling the ball from the base of the scrum. He is cheerful, laughing, happy, the youngest son, the sunny lad who brings lightens a room with his entrance. Sometimes a family is not a real family until its last member arrives and the zip is then finally made secure, top and bottom. That was Kevin. With him, the Teevan family unit was finally sealed. Long before he went off to war, they'd already nearly lost him in Dun Laoghaire swimming pool, which was fed by the sea. Someone pulled out the stop-cock while he was in the water, and he was sucked down into the long sluice channel and onto the grievous rocks beyond. Yet he survived, the laughing jokester always. His wartime enlistment was a big step. The Teevans were cautious Irish nationalists, not usually the kind to seek a commission in the British army.

He departed for war, and within the year was dead, killed in Sierra Leone by polio as he awaited embarkation for Burma. He died bravely, giving clinical descriptions of the symptoms of his approaching end, that science might better understand how the disease works. The family put a death notice in *The Irish Times*, stating his military rank as a captain in the Royal Army Medical Corps, and giving the Myers personal address at Mobhi Road as his. Shortly afterwards, Fionain Lynch, a politician and old friend of my father, contacted Dad to say that the Dublin Tramway Company was being taken over by the state, and Dad's job – hitherto guaranteed and secure – was now about to be secretly advertised in the government newspaper, *The Irish Press*, but in the Irish language only, which of course Dad didn't speak. This was to ensure he didn't even see the advert. So Dad then applied for his own job, and after he was duly interviewed – in English – the position was then given (as it was always going to be) to the newly graduated son-in-law of the minister for agriculture. Aged forty-three, the father of three children, honest Dr William George Myers was out of work.

Dad of course wrote a strongly worded letters of protest – this in a land where public probity was as scant as lunar lichen. Fionain Lynch bore the discreet offer back to him, that he would be looked after and given a medical dispensary in County Monaghan if he did one of two things. One was to join the government party of Fianna Fáil (the fine fellows whose leaders two decades before were gunmen, and who had just now shafted him), or even just to shut up and join the Knights of Columbanus, the Irish Catholic freemasonry. By this time, he should have understood that whenever a blood-and-cordite political gang like Fianna Fáil offers you two options, you really should take a third: you do both.

But Dad did neither, and instead, in the very middle of a world war – somehow unnoticed between the Battle of Kursk on the Eastern Front and Operation Husky, the Allied landings in Sicily – he embarked upon his own little war against the Irish government with a series of deeply ill-advised letters to all in authority. Thus perished Dad's career as a GP in Ireland.

My mother's older sister Enid was a doctor, though of the strictly non-practising variety, living in Devon and married to a rich and elderly Scot named Ebenezer Orr, poor fucker. Though she always professed her loyalty to Britain, she was stoutly resisting a British government order compelling all non-practising doctors to fill any local medical vacancies. Thus Dad's misfortune was her deliverance, for she was able to conjure this compliant Irishman, quite out of the ether, to do the work she didn't want to do.

So it was that Dad got a job as a wartime locum in Exmouth, near where she lived. He went over first, to be followed some months later by my mother, their three small children, a dog and, for some reason, my grandmother. Thus, the Myers family reversed what are almost universal human practices, and moved from a neutral country into a belligerent one, with a U-boat drill on the Liverpool ferry. The journey from there to Exmouth, on blacked-out trains crowded with troops bound for war, took days.

A series of subsidiary events, whose admittedly enormous significance lies in their conclusion, led my parents to Leicester, where I was born at 1 pm on Palm Sunday, 30 March 1947, to be followed twenty minutes later by my sister Margaret. So soon afterwards Mum prevailed upon him finally to buy somewhere in the city and to settle down. With unerring skill they found 17 Medina Road. We were now to be the Myers family of Leicester, and England was to be our home.

Three

AT THE AGE of six Maggy and I left Hazeldean for Nativity Convent in Evington, on the far side of the city, and two bus rides away. The journey meant nothing to us, for any apprehension about strange men was utterly absent from our lives. I instantly liked the Convent, for my class contained only three boys, John Lennon, Alan Wells and myself. The former's father was a tea factor who had moved from Liverpool, which raises all sorts of interesting possibilities. And of course, there were many, many girls – a sumptuous plenitude! – with their own cloakroom; what a place of mystery.

At the Convent I learnt for the first time that some adults actually want to be unkind to children. There was an Irish teacher there who was cunning and clever, and she hated me. She used to hit me secretly, and twist my arm, but never in front of the class. On the other hand, there was also the sweetest teacher, Sister St Clement, whose kindliness was of a saintly variety, and recognized as such by all the children.

One day Maggy felt unwell, so I travelled to school alone. Gazing through the bus window, I saw a sign on an office window saying *Invisible Police*. Invisible police! What a wonderful job, and exactly what I would become when I was grown up! I could see no policemen going in and out, because they were invisible! Why, once I was an invisible policeman like them, I could even saunter into the girls' cloakrooms and watch them getting changed. The only question was, how could I join? (I didn't tell Maggy about my planned intrusion into the girls' changing-room, for there are some things one doesn't share with a sister).

When Maggy was better, on our next journey home, I joyfully pointed out the headquarters of The Invisible Police to her. It was not for the first time in our lives, or the last, that Maggy's superior learning triumphed. The headquarters of the surreptitious constabulary was in fact an insurance company, which was offering *Invincible Policies*.

THE DAYS of the Greystones family holidays had come to an end. The month away, plus the cost of hiring a locum for that time, was too much for the Myers budget – not least because the locums could usually be relied on to steal anything not nailed down in the family home. These seemed to be troubled creatures, drawn from the feckless post-war ranks of the unsettled, the alcoholic, the slightly shell-shocked. Moreover, to leave one's patients in the hands of deranged vagrants for an entire month seemed vaguely un-Hippocratic.

That, anyway, was the plan. One day Dad called me into his workshop, where I often went to watch him making his angling flies, or fiddling with molten solder in some doomed little engineering scheme.

'Would you like to go back to Ireland this year?'

'I thought we weren't going there any more.'

'We are. But just you, me and Bill.'

Bill was my brother, eight years older than me, and therefore almost a member of another family. Why us two? I don't know. Certainly, my mother didn't know what Dad had in mind, for it was I who broke the news to her that Dad, Bill and I were going to Ireland, but no one else was. She stalked into the surgery and she and Dad had a terrible, terrible row, which changed nothing.

To my mind, partitioned from adult reality, we had a lovely trip, first by train to Holyhead, and then by ferry. We stayed with my Aunt Ellie, and Uncle Ted, and her Aunt Margaret, a handsome and gaunt old woman aged about 170, with her black weeds and her black, black staring eyes, a single glare from which could stampede lions. Almost every on the hour, I feasted on sausages and rashers and brown bread and butter, yes butter, which I had never tasted before, and lashings of that mysterious Irish phenomenon, red lemonade, full of life-giving tartrazine, while the inscrutable black eyes rested on me, like a shaman examining my forebears. Around the corner lived Dad's sister Pat, a jolly fat woman, and her husband Martin, the sage old stone mason, and their delicious daughter Breda, a couple of years older than me, with whom I fell instantly in love.

Instead of going home via the ferry, we went to Dublin airport. Dad had booked a flight to Manchester. It must have been hideously expensive, but I was beside myself with near-hysterical excitement. Me. In a plane!

In the cafeteria, yes, aged seven, I spotted a really beautiful woman. She had a wasp-waist dress, with a wide belt, her lipstick was a full red, and most dazzling of all, she wore white gloves. I prayed that she was on the same plane as us. She was, but I couldn't see her from my seat. I lost sight of her again at Manchester Airport, and dolefully I went with Dad and Bill to the airport bus into the city centre. My heart thumped like a warrant-server's knock when I clambered aboard, for there sitting at the back, on the raised level over the luggage compartment, was the love of my life. While Dad and Bill sat down near the front, I went to the back, to sit near her. She turned and smiled at me, and I suffered a small coronary occlusion. I pretended not to watch her through the journey, but through the corner of my eyes, I was gazing obsessively at her.

'Goodbye, you cheeky young devil,' she whispered when we got to Manchester. She laid a gloved hand on my cheek, and then walked out of my life. Dad was at the bottom of the steps waiting for me when I alighted.

'Found yourself a girlfriend, I see, young fellow me lad,' he smiled. He was quietly delighted, and I was not exactly displeased. I think that in regard to women, and a fondness for, my father was not unlike me.

Next item on the agenda of paternal eccentricity was a fishing holiday for the same three of us at Stoke Dry Reservoir in Rutland. This was where we sometimes went to be bitten by flies on hot Sunday afternoons in the summer. Bill and Dad and I were now to spend an entire week there. Bill did not fish, and nor did I. Dad fished, but usually fishlessly. Nonetheless, he had hired a lakeside caravan for us.

The caravan introduced me to several new life experiences, all of them life-diminishing, the most harrowing of which was the chemical toilet. This consisted of a seat that opened directly onto a tank containing a foul liquid chemical. It had not been emptied from the caravan's previous tenants, and the surface of the liquid was packed with floating waste, like life-jacketed corpses from a sunken liner. But as I soon discovered, the dense population of such detritus in no way diminished either the volume or the velocity of the splashback. No matter how hard I tried, no matter the altitude I chose to operate from, I was always rewarded with a solids-rich return of service, right into the very point of departure of my own modest contribution to the burly sea below. After most visits, I usually felt that I had probably gained more than I had shed.

Daily, I watched various opened but unfinished bottles of milk turning sour, as clouds of spores wafted through the caravan in an enquiring mist. Milk clearly had to be at least 70 per cent streptomycin and 90 per cent rainbow before Dad would throw it out. However, he was not entirely indifferent to health – he was a GP, after all – which is why he had suspended two flypapers from the caravan ceiling. A few flies, perhaps weakened by age, did indeed stick permanently on these sticky strips. But the paper strips were mostly unable to detain any able-bodied flies, which accordingly slid slowly down before dripping off, like hairy, armour-plated raindrops.

Thus in time the caravan came to be populated by scores of semi-ambulant bluebottles hauling their gummy limbs and their broken wings after them. Uncovered foodstuffs were soon festooned with the walking wounded, furiously stroking everything with their proboscis. At night I would wake up to the sense of sticky-footed insects labouring over my face, looking for my nostrils. So I would lie back, pinching my nose, as their tiny feet tapped and enquired. In the morning, I could actually feel the tacky trail of bluebottle hoof prints etched on my lips.

There was no shower, no bath, and no way of keeping clean. A visit to the chemical latrine would start the day, with the floating mementos from our different alimentary pasts companionably shouldering one another in the stilly oils. A frank exchange of materials would then follow. Cleansing operations to conclude this merry little interlude would be performed with the dear old Jeyes toilet sheets, but frankly, I might just as well have been using the flypaper.

We spent the day in the rowing boat on the placid mosquito factory of Stoke Dry. Dad caught two tiny slippery things that flapped and smelt of fish. He unhooked them and threw them back. Later, on the road leading from the lake, rabbits were dying of this new disease, myxomatosis. Dad wondered if he would finish them off as they lay in his path, but he simply wasn't able to. He was a doctor, after all. So he drove carefully around these baffled, blind and doomed creatures, whom I rather envied, and safely back to the caravan.

In the evening we smeared runny butter onto slices of stale bread, followed by body temperature sardines, which were usually just fine since their tins had only been opened a couple of days before. Awakened from their comas by the strange smell, large crippled flies came limping across the table with outstretched paws. However, I should not exaggerate the monotony of the table d'hôte, for once we had Spam, which plopped out warmly from the inverted can with the greasy ease of a cubic piglet from a well-practised sow.

One evening I was sitting outside, possibly contemplating an early death, when I spotted a great glow in the distant sky. A fire! A massive gigantic colossal fire! Dear Christ alive, there was almost nothing I loved more than a good blaze. So I got Dad up from his bed so as to drive me towards this huge inferno: why, if God was good, maybe I would even see people leaping to their death or burning alive! Their screams! Their flaming limbs!

Dad and I and an incredulous Bill (who had been forcibly dragged away from his night-time reading) set off in the Vanguard in pursuit of the fire. But the closer we should have come to it, the more distant it mysteriously became, like a perpetually receding oasis. We finally arrived a phone kiosk, which inspired in me a quite brilliant solution.

'Dad, Dad, Dad,' I urged, 'ring 999, and say you're a doctor, and you think there's a huge great fire, and poor innocent people are burning to death, we've got to get there in a hurry and save their lives. Quick quick quick!'

Dad got out and made the call as I writhed impatiently beside him.

'I see,' said Dad in a low voice, after reporting this abominable inferno. 'I see. I'm sorry for troubling you.'

He turned to me. 'Well, we've been making right eejits of ourselves. It seems we've been chasing the steel works in Corby.'

That summer we took our first family trip to the Welsh seaside resort of Criccieth. It was a lovely holiday, the forerunner of many, and since few things bore so much as an account of happy families having a happy time, we shall move swiftly on to our return homeward through the Welsh mountains. The roof lid was open, and I was, as usual, standing perched on the back of the front seats, with most of my body above the car, shooting at things. Dad was driving in low gear as we wound downward the steep slopes, and the resulting noise sounded just like a police siren in an American TV drama.

'Do it again, Dad, make the cop-car noise again,' I would shout down to him as we breasted a rise, a steep decline before us. He would accordingly put the Vanguard in an unnaturally low gear, and the interior metals of the transmission would howl in protest as the entire downhill weight of the car, plus eight Myerses, their bags and their buckets and spades, bore down on the tortured clutch-plates. Inevitably, on a steep hillside outside Llanngollen, the poor gearbox finally exploded and the Vanguard crawled to the side of the road where it sighed ferrously and died. Thus it was that we found themselves stranded in the middle of the Welsh countryside on a Saturday afternoon, effectively carless, but by God, not bagless.

Like refugees in France the year after 17 Medina Road was completed, and all bearing baggage, we tottered to a distant garage, which was of course closed. A tow vehicle was finally summoned and the car was retrieved. It was beyond immediate repair, its entire clutch and gearbox in shreds. Darkness rapidly fell. We made our broken way homeward, first by overloaded Bedford van to a railway station, and then by various, various trains to many, many different platforms smelling of cold and coal and homelessness, and finally to Great Central Railway Station, Leicester, on that evil, winnowed and taxiless Sabbath dawn, from where, beneath the weight of our various bags, we limped and hobbled to Medina Road, where we found that the stand-in doctor had already fled, taking with him all the family linen.

Four

THAT AUTUMN Maggy and I went our separate ways educationally, and remained so divided for the rest of our lives. I departed to Christ the King, a state-run Catholic school, while Maggy remained at the more socially exclusive convent. I found school easy, and I was pretty good at most things. The only really troublesome teacher was a Miss Lavelle, who had dyed hair and a club foot, and, like Miss Lynch, a tendency to clobber children for no apparent reason. Like my earlier tormenter, she too was Irish. The children called her The Limper Lavelle, but not affectionately.

Moreover, I can say with some certainty that in the ability to generate fear without saying a word, alongside the figures of Mao, Stalin and Beria stands the figure of Miss Bratt, headmistress of Christ the King. I give her no first name, because clearly her parents had lacked the nerve to give her one. No matter: she was an extraordinarily successful headmistress, as shown by the relative lack of corporal punishment in what was quite a tough, working-class school.

I was now in childhood, not infancy. I'd already had my Catholic sacraments, my first confession of sins, and my First Communion. Like almost every child, I had no sins to confess, and so I had fabricated a couple of fibs to fill the unnervingly virtuous vacuum in the confessional. The First Communion that followed the next day was invested with rather more awe. I had been told that I must not let the communion wafer touch my teeth (that was a sin) and I must not chew it (that was an even greater sin). I had entered a world of entirely invented sins – earth-movers boring tunnels for the heavier traffic still to come.

My younger brother Johnny was now old enough to play with Maggy and me and Mark. We invented something called the chasing game, in which he would run after us with a stick. Then he would again chase us, and if he could, touch us with the stick. Our garden circled the house, but there was a hedge at right angles to one side, which reached to the boundary fence and prevented 360-degree movement round the house. But we had burrowed a small hole through it and our evaders' trick was to race to the hedge and run through the hole.

Susan Padstow asked us one evening if she could join us. I was against any girls joining the game because it was largely a boys' game – Maggy, of course, didn't count as a girl. Mark was initially against it too. Finally, on Mark's suggestion, Susan agreed to take her knickers off. So Johnny would chase us across the garden to the hedge, at which point Mark and I grew curiously lame as we approached it. This allowed Susan to hurtle into the hole in the hedge first, and Mark and I would take turns in following this damsel in undress as she burrowed through on all fours. After a long and very pleasant evening, with many splendid vistas before us, Susan went home. But the silly girl forget to put her knickers on, and seven kinds of hell followed when Mrs Padstow discovered her daughter had been out running around with boys, but without underwear. Henceforth, we continued to play the chasing game, but the landscape thereafter was never quite as beguiling as it had been on that summer evening.

Our games empire now included the allotments, once visible on Hitler's snapshots but since degenerated into a weed-covered wasteland. These were our 'lotties', our paradise, with apple trees, wild raspberries, rhubarb, cowboys, Indians, lions and tigers.

One day, Mark and I were playing there when he shouted excitedly for me to come over to him.

'Ey up, Kev, look a' tha',' he whispered, pointing at a large object on the ground. It was an absolutely huge turd, which in Leicester child parlance was known as a 'bob'.

'Tha' were a roigh' big dog wa' dún tha',' observed Mark gravely.

'Hmm. That wasn't a dog,' said Sherlock here. 'I rather think that it must have come from a human being.'

'Oo ya beauty!' cried Mark, reeling in wonder. We had to spread this important news as quickly as possible. We raced back to Mark's mother.

'Ey úp Mam! Me and Kev were just down the lotties!' Mark declared excitedly. 'And we found this bob, and it were dead big, and Kev reckons it were YOOMAN!'

Mrs Patterson remained curiously unmoved by this epic discovery. However, she was not always so stoic in the face of the little dramas that Mark and I presented to her. One afternoon, the pair of us were playing in his back garden, while his parents and his Aunt Elsie were sitting in the sun.

'Ooh ah'd lúv an ice-cream, ah would,' said Elsie. 'It's tharr 'o'.' (that hot).

'Ooh ah, it is an' all,' said Mr Patterson, that large, gruff and charmless man with his huge bald head. 'Ey up, Mark, you and Kev goo dahn to Mr Baxter's and gerr us three ice cream cornets, and ge' one each for yourselves.' He turned to his wife. 'Oo ah say, 'ave you any change?'

'Oh ah shoulda guessed it'd cúmm to this.'

Mr Baxter, the owner of the local sweet-shop, was a wizened, grasping miser with a bald pointy head, sharp yellow teeth and small pink eyes. In my early childhood, when farthings (worth about a tenth of a modern cent) still circulated, he would always insist on the last farthing being paid. Mrs Patterson grumpily opened her near-empty purse and fished out some coins, from which she counted exactly the right amount into Mark's hand. The pair of us then, as always, ran to the shops. We passed a newsagents, and I saw a comic I wanted. I decided to spend my ice-cream money on that.

Later, as we ran out of Mr Baxter's, one of Mark's ice-creams fell from its cornet. 'Búgger,' he whispered, and the pair of us then ran back to the waiting adults. Mark handed his two surviving ice-creams to Elsie and to Mr Patterson. I handed mine towards Mrs Patterson but even as she reached for it, the ice-cream toppled out of the cone and into the flowerbed beside her.

'Look what you're doing, ya daft thing!' she cried. 'You'll ave to goo wirrout nah, an' ah'll 'ave yourn.'

I handed her the comic. 'I'm very sorry, but that's what I spent my money on.'

'What! A comic! You spent me blúddy ice-cream money on a blúddy COMIC?' She scowled, opened her purse, and gave me her very last thruppence. 'Now go an' get me anúther one. An' 'úrry now, ah dúnt want to be eating mahn on me own.'

I ran with due speed to and from Mr Sharp's, arriving with the fresh ice-cream intact, while the others were happily still devouring theirs. Deeply relieved, I handed my cargo over towards Mrs Patterson. Just as she reached for it, the very last ice-cream fell to its doom.

'Good God!' she wailed brokenly. ''E's dúnn it agen!'

No, not me, but my fatal genes. I truly was my father's son.

Dad had a strict policy that we should be very polite to everyone, especially the less fortunate. This included Sheldon, a shabby lunatic who would regularly stand at the corner of Medina Road and Buckminster Road in an old tweed cap and stinking overcoat, talking gibberish. On one crimson morning, he had cacklingly tried to amputate his fingers, in public at that junction, with the edge of an open tin can. Other children mocked him, but on orders from Dad, we Little Ones were always courteous to him. The most difficult object for this regimen of respect was Mark's cousin and near neighbour, Pip Chumley, who was a little older than us. He was a fearsome, pop-eyed, squinting, muscular little brute, with wire-framed spectacles halfway down his perpetually dribbling nose. But it was not only his appearance that made Pip the terror that he was, but also his pet stick, which he always carried. With his spare hand, he either picked his nose, wiping his discoveries on the shirt of the nearest child, or he kept it down the front of his trousers, where he usually found an occupation for it. On one spectacular occasion, this splendid young citizen emptied his bowels in the gutter outside 17 Medina Road, glaring round him like a mother hen laying some very precious eggs.

Dad's injunctions on politeness even embraced the toughs from nearby Gene Drive, who actually wore jeans every day (a sure sign of delinquency). Like most Leicester people, they were uncertain about their voiced aspirants.

'You're dead posh you are, dead lah-di-dah,' sneered one of them to me.

'No I'm not. I'm dead ordinary, actually.'

"Ark 'ow you talk, you say hactually!'

'No I don't, I say, actually actually.'

'And your mam and dad, they're dead posh an' all.'

'No, I'm sorry, they're not.'

'Yeah they are. They dún't say, "oo yer fúcker, and oo yer búgger and oo yer fúckin cúnt", like me mam and dad do. Your mam and dad, they say, "oo yah foohkah and oo yah boohgah and oo yah foohking cahnt".'

But Gene Drive thugs were nothing compared to the hard little boys from Woodgate's terraced houses two hundred yards away from our home, who if they had any young would probably have eaten them. Some of them even smoked in public, pinching out a half-finished cigarette and putting the butt behind the ear.

MILK in those days came on horse-drawn floats every morning, and during the school holidays, boys would scramble onto the float to help the milkman on his round. The high point of such a trip would be to witness a horse having a bob, from just inches away: such joy! The bread van came once a week, as did the Corona minerals electric float. The aristocrat of delivery vehicles was the monthly ginger-pop truck, which was purpose-built, with tiered shelves for carrying the expensive stone jars. The primacy of ginger beer began to be threatened by the arrival of the 'ginger-pop plant', which had no apparent commercial motive. Children started cultivating this strange fungal growth in bottles with ginger, sugar and water. After a couple of days the result would be a naturally carbonated ginger pop, which was nearly as good as the lorry-delivered stuff in jars, and almost free, so ginger pop became the staple mid-morning drink at school. Suddenly, the ginger-pop delivery man was almost out of business.

Delivered produce apart, all household goods were bought locally in the shops at the bottom of Buckminster Road, the nearest shop, a hundred yards away at the far end of the lotties, being Titchley's the chemist. The sublimely named Mr Titchley was about five feet in height. His son Tim, however (probably begot by a very large and very stupid postman), was a giant, about three years older than us twins, but with half our individual IQs, and twice our weight combined at a time when fatness was very unusual. Every childhood in those days had one fat inhabitant. We had Tim.

Happily, these shops represented a territorial and class barrier beyond which the Woodgate Mau Mau seemed reluctant to cross, so leaving the lotties as the primary possession of Medina Road. This was our two acres of playground, where Indians uttered their final whoops and tigers were manfully choked to death. One Saturday afternoon, when no patients would ever call, Dad answered a knock on the door. It was Tim Titchley.

'Good afternoon, Dr Myers,' this obese child wheezed.

'Hello Tim, how can I help you? Are you all right?'

'Yes, thank you very much Dr Myers. I was wondering if you'd like a box of matches.'

'Of course, Tim.'

The boy thanked him profusely, and handing him the matches, waddled off, breaking into something that could almost be called a run.

Some time later we heard fire-engine bells. Brilliant! I hurried out to investigate, hoping to see the nearby shops being consumed by an inferno. Instead, I found our lotties seriously on fire. A score of firemen were fighting the blaze, some moving across the scrubland in a line, beating the wall of flames with wet sacking. Together, they managed to control the blaze just before it reached the long wooden Myers fence. The police came later and announced that they were sure it was a case of arson, but of course, they never found the culprit. How could they? The Billy Bunter responsible had, the moment he realized his game with matches had got out of out of control, fled home – but only after planting all the incriminating evidence on the First Citizen of Myètopia.

Dad always fiddling with other new inventions in his workshop. One was a complex contraption that would take a patient's temperature and blood pressure simultaneously, and which involved a large bath of mercury. Of course, he soon spilled this all over the surgery floor, so the two of us spent half an afternoon chasing the scattered gallon of quicksilver, which proved just as elusive as the trout. Dad decided that we should use glass pipettes to suck the mercury up, which we did. If I'd been suffering from syphilis that morning, I was completely cured by evening.

Another invention was a pneumatic jack that would effortlessly raise a car with a flat tyre by using the extra pressure from the spare. He proudly demonstrated it to me one Saturday afternoon. He connected the jack to the spare tyre, and as promised, the car rose without sound or effort. Dad then removed the wheel from the hub. This needless tempting of fate seems to have triggered the betrayal instinct of the jack, for it promptly began to hoist the car even higher, by inhaling all the air from the spare tyre. Once it too was also flat, the jack then collapsed, as did the car, driving the wheel hub deep into the drive. Dad had, quite brilliantly, created a device that could transform the slight drama of a flat tyre into the personal calamity of a marooned car with two flat tyres and a wheel hub embedded in tarmac.

On another occasion, he rightly and (considering the mobile phone was then in the utterly unforeseeable future) even presciently, divined that the car lighter could be used for other purposes – in his case, such as powering another jack. Being a zealous smoker, he decided to retain the lighter function by inserting a home-made adaptor with two outlets. Then he managed to stick his thumb deep into the cigarette lighter, burning it hideously. I was not to know that smell again until I met it in Belfast, where the IRA regularly did to entire people what Dad had done to the tip of his thumb.

One November he took an unusual interest in our preparations for Guy Fawkes Night, which until the more recent arrival of the grey squirrel of Hallowe'en was just about the only widely observed folk and entirely native festival in English life. The Little Ones usually saved up our pocket money from September onwards to buy fireworks; however, on this particular night he presented us with a huge rocket that had cost a guinea, or twenty-one whole shillings. You could buy a normal rocket for sixpence, one forty-fourth of the price of Dad's monster and frankly, being an expert in such matters, I compared it rather favourably with a Hawker Hunter (FGA) 9 air-to-ground missile.

Ordinary rockets were launched from bottles sunk into the ground. This beast, however, had to be secured to a firm upright mounting. We had such a thing: the gate-less gatepost in the front of the garage. The local Guy Fawkes bonfire always took place on the lotties, when all boundaries vanished. Thus the uncouth simians from Woodgate were permitted to shamble up before the big night, dragging surplus old beds, armchairs, roof joists and unwanted grandmothers to dump on the intended inferno. On the night itself, throngs of people would gather in reverential silence until by some social alchemy, a silent consensual cue was reached, and the fire was lit.

This November evening, we watched as a huge heap of junk was transformed into a mesmerizing bonfire before we returned home for the highlight of the night: Dad had improvised a bracket on the gatepost, which stood only a few feet from the edge of the lotties. The bonfire – now surrounded by a couple of hundred people – was about fifty yards away from us. He lowered the rocket vertically into the bracket, ordered us all to stand back, and then lit the magical blue-touch paper, before withdrawing, as according to Socratic law.

The rocket began to cough and splutter with monstrous promise, but just as it was about to depart spaceward, the top point of the holding bracket broke free and the whole unit swivelled at right angles round its base, causing the rocket to point horizontally towards the crowds of Guy Fawkes revellers.

'Jesus Christ Almighty!' cried Dad.

With a huge bang, the rocket erupted from its moorings and headed directly into the crowd. Many, if not most, would have been on Dad's National Health Service panel: he was, apparently, about to conduct a massacre of his own patients. Next moment, as we watched in horror, the flaming projectile had vanished in their midst. Would we be dragging the broken bodies of Dad's victims into his surgery for him to try yet more of his magic upon? What precisely does a doctor say in such circumstances? And equally, had the British Medical Association ever formulated a policy for dealing with a doctor who had first slain or maimed his patients outside his surgery, before treating them inside it?

By an utter miracle, the flaming missile navigated its way through some tiny gap in the dancing mill of locals, but it could not possibly miss Titchley's chemist's shop. Naturally, however, instead of exploding harmlessly against the wall, as a less Myètopian missile would certainly have done, the rocket flew directly through the single pharmacy window. A moment later, it exploded with a huge flash and a bang that echoed over the crowds. But by this time, the entire Myers tribe had prudently vanished back inside our home, on our knees and singing psalms.

The next day tiny Mr Titchley indignantly asked Dad to sign a petition against any more bonfires on the allotments – vandals the night before had nearly burnt his shop down, he declared, and his pharmacy had been gutted. What! Dad reeled in horrified amazement: how shocking. However, surely Mr Titchley could see that it was not possible for an Irish Catholic doctor to interfere in a festival that was so dear to so many Protestant English hearts. Thereafter, Dad's interest in autumnal rocketry waned somewhat.

However, sometimes we applied Dad's larger moral injunctions about showing goodness to others applied only fitfully. One day, when the Little Ones, Susan and Mark were playing in our back garden, a rain of half bricks began to fall upon us, accompanied by whoops of triumph. Only one boy would have the evil forethought to establish such an arsenal of missiles, and the strength to hurl them, all accompanied such convincing King Kong imitations. Pip of course. We had endured too much for too long.

We thought long and hard. It was – I confess in all modesty – I who came up with the only logical solution. We had to dispose of Pip. We couldn't simply beat him to death: he was a practised, stick-wielding thug. We needed to be cunning. Mum had warned us never to eat cooking apples, assuring us they were very dangerous uncooked; in other words, poisonous. So I painted a biliously green cooking apple a bright and sumptuous red, against the time when Pip would strike again.

We were splashing around in wellies in the lagoon in front of the surgery when Pip arrived, squinting evilly, and looking very, very menacing. I got my retaliation in first.

'Hiyah, Pip. Would you like an apple?'

With one hand foraging inside his trousers, industriously entertaining himself as always, and with his trusty stick in his other hand, he grunted 'Ooh ah.'

'Good! I'll be back in a minute.'

I was back in less than that. 'There you are Pip: a Pippin apple, just for you.'

He begrudgingly withdrew his hand from his trousers and took the apple. He sniffed it, and glared around at us, before grunting and eating it in about five huge bites. We waited for him to die, or at least faint. He did neither.

'Roigh't,' he grunted, satisfied. 'Wa' game we gonna play next?'

He then proceeded to chase us all through the Myers lagoon like an inexhaustible hippopotamus. I was about to offer him Susan Padstow, in her sumptuous entirety, in exchange for Johnny, whom he was enthusiastically drowning, when the arrival of Pip's mother rendered such stratagems unnecessary. He vanished soon afterwards into an asylum for Sexually Deranged Axe Murderers, and when last heard of had become a merchant banker.

ONE MORNING at school, a student teacher introduced herself to me. She knew my older sister Ann; they were at college together. She solemnly shook my hand. She was astoundingly pretty, with lovely arching eyebrows, like my girlfriend on the airport bus. The mid-morning break was next, with PE to follow. A classmate, Peter Keegan, came up to me while I was running around the playground.

'Ey úp! You see that teacher what you was talking to at the end of class? She's rúddy well getting changed in storeroom for PE!'

He ran over to the high window of the storeroom, and jumped up so that he could briefly see into it.

He landed and turned to me, his eyes wide.

'Oo ya beauty,' he whispered. 'She's took 'er rúddy skirt off.'

I needed no more prompting. From right beneath the high window, I did a standing jump as high as I could, and rose beautifully and vertically so that my face was far above the window. Yes, I could see in! Yes, there was Miss, bending down, bare beneath the waist! Yes, and there was her bum! As my head reached the apogee, the student teacher looked up and round, her sports shorts around her knees, and wide-eyed, spotted my head hovering briefly above the windowsill, while I, equally wide-eyed, absorbed all her near-naked loveliness.

Even as I began my descent, I took with me a mental image of her horrified face (which remains with me still). I hit the ground. Lord love a duck! This was a friend of my sister's! And she had clearly seen it was me, catching her half naked! Yes, with her bare bum! Suddenly, I saw a solution to my dilemma. What if that leap, which had brought me soaring above the windowsill, was actually innocent, and that was how I normally proceeded around the playground? That is to say, I suffered from the opposite of a limp, namely, an impediment that was a convulsive leap? She would then realize I was a cripple who had seen her only by accident! So I spent the rest of the break bounding around the playground, in a series of huge, palsied hops. And by God, it seems to have worked, because to this day, I never heard another word about it.

Christ the King was a very orderly school, and the symptoms of imminent chaos only appeared gradually. One day a couple of girls had tried to stand on their heads in the middle of the playground, without a wall to lean against, and without tucking in their skirts. Much of the school had gathered to watch. After balancing for a half a minute, effectively just in their knickers, they both fell flat on their backs, and instead of crying, they laughed hysterically.

'Betcha you wouldn't do that in your nude,' grunted a boy.

'Wun't ah?' said one, and discarding her knickers, promptly did.

During the mid-morning break a few days later, two of the best-behaved boys in the entire school, Cedric and Robin, lit cigarettes in the playground, like Woodgate lads, right under the eyes of an incredulous Miss Lavelle.

'Put out those cigarettes this second,' she screeched.

'Ey up,' said one of the choirboys out of the corner of his mouth, 'Ah reckon old Limper's got the 'ump.' He nipped the end of the cigarette, and put the stub behind his ear. The panic-stricken Miss Lavelle promptly hobbled off to seek assistance from Miss Bratt. After the break, Nigel Watkin, clearly destined to be the very first St Nigel, rose in class and enquired of the class teacher, Mr Blacklock: 'Please sir, w'y are you called Mr Blacklock, w'en you 'aven't got a single black lock on your 'ole blúddy head?'

Mr Blackrock had served in the Western Desert, and when he caned a boy – which was not often – that boy stayed caned. So goody-goody Nigel Watkin got four of the best.

Blacklock stood glaring, hoping to see signs of abjection contrition. Young Watkin was bound for the priesthood; he would surely break now.

'Well, Watkin?' asked Blacklock. 'What have you to say for yourself?'

'Ah've 'ad farts that 'urt more,' replied the future saint.

He was the first and only boy that Blacklock ever sent to Miss Bratt. Matters became rather more critical when the boys were told to depart the assembly hall, leaving just the girls there. They joined us later in class. At first, none of them would tell us what had happened in our absence, until a girl named Tina Brown relented. Apparently one of the girls, she whispered, and using her own bob, had smeared 'Miss Bratt is a cunt' on a toilet door. It says something of the awe in which our headmistress was held that even amid such scatological and insurrectionary daubings, she retained her honorific.

Nonetheless, this was truly sensational stuff. Christ the King was falling apart! So where would all this end? It was time to call in the hero of El Alamein. Mr Blacklock. He managed to connect the eruptions of disorder either with the end of breaktime, or just afterwards, when children had been drinking their own home-made ginger pop. It turned out that the ginger pop plant was actually a yeast, which had been brewed in its bottles for too long. Instead of just producing carbon dioxide, it had generated ginger-flavoured moonshine, resulting in a mini-epidemic of drunkenness amongst a group of normally docile ten-year olds. After that, home-made ginger pop was outlawed, the local ginger-pop delivery man breathed a sigh of relief, and Christ the King was able to revert to a more traditional interpretation of a Catholic educational ethos.

Five

UNLIKE MUM, Dad was not religious. What his actual beliefs were, I cannot say for sure. He was silent, almost inscrutable, on such matters. He generally did not attend the 8.30 am Mass with us. Whenever he did, the moment that he felt a sermon was lasting even a second too long, he would take out his car keys and rattle them, clearing his throat purposefully at the errant clergyman. The Little Ones would of course turn scarlet and hide our faces, desperately hoping no one would think we were with him.

It was at my mother's urging that I became an altar boy for the Friday morning Mass at Christ the King. This was a job – part valet, part religious celebrant – for which I had no natural talent. Fortunately, there was one regular altar boy, Kevin Mansfield, a youthful Jeeves who could recite all the responses by heart. This other Kevin M. was red-haired, intelligent, religious and popular. His RAF father had been shot down during the war and he had never recovered from his years as a POW. He spent his day hunched by the coal fire in his tiny terraced house, where he treated his TB-damaged lungs by chain-smoking untipped Craven A cigarettes. Not merely were these good and strong, probably killing all known germs (as he had once explained to me) but they also guaranteed a good bronchial clear-out.

Not everything had the life-prolonging qualities of cigarettes. Coins were seen as a real threat to one's health as the vector of polio, truly the fatal epidemic of my childhood. At Christ the King we became pretty polio-literate, disputing which coins were likely to be more deadly, and even having arguments over the merits of the Salk anti-polio vaccine from America compared to the British polio vaccine. These were conducted on largely jingoistic lines: the British vaccine was of course better, but the American was cheaper. Typical Yanks, always looking to save money – but their vaccine didn't have the class that the British had.

The dirtiest and smelliest of the Christ the King boys, alas, were usually from first-generation Irish families. These tended to be in the B-stream. The only boy in my class who smelt, Dermot Browne, was also both Irish and violent. Gaunt, undernourished and wearing stinking hand-me-downs, he was always getting into, and worse, winning, fights. He filled me with real worry: for what if he picked a fight with me? But instead, he very decently always chose to fight boys of his own social status, which to my mind was a complete vindication of the English class system. But he made a grave mistake in picking on Peter Keegan (obviously also Irish), who gave him a really sound, turn-your-eyes-away thrashing – so much so that I actually felt sorry for him. Some time later Miss Bratt announced at morning assembly that we were all going to be praying for young Patrick Browne, Dermot's younger brother, who had contracted polio. And pray we unfailingly did, because we knew that some terrors were of the imagination, and some were real, and this was one of the latter. What had hitherto been like a terrifying story from the Brothers Grimm was now a sinister reality in our midst.

The next morning when I arrived at school no one was playing. Children had gathered in silent groups, looking frightened. Patrick Browne was dead. This was quite shocking, an appalling insight into what surely should be an adult monopoly.

We all prayed for Patrick Browne's little soul. This was my first death, and I wondered what had happened that had turned him from a living boy into a corpse. A weeping Dermot was back in class the next week. Some days later, a pretty young girl in a junior class whose name I didn't even know also died of polio. This was terrible. Who next? It could be any of us. Death had arrived in the school, and was in every class. Yet in all this fear, other and quite dreadful priorities asserted themselves. For the dead girl was middle class, and Miss Bratt announced that the school was going to erect a window in her memory, though none was to be erected for poor Patrick. Even though in my own little way, I was an ineffable little snob, I also knew that this was very wrong.

However, the Brownes' Irishness was not the reason why their lad got no memorial. For when Christ the King had a fundraising week for Hungarian refugees, the proceeds were handed to the Lord Mayer of Leicester by the most suitably grand little boy in the school, Kevin Myers. I have a photograph of the occasion still, and frankly, I was a winsome little fucker.

Dad was always content for us to find our own level socially: if we mixed with working-class children, so be it. Mum, however, was determined to make us all very middle class. And so once a month I caught the bus into town to Belvoir Street. No working-class boy ever had the carefully angled fringe across the forehead that I got there. After I paid my one shilling and thruppence at the cash desk, I would solemnly return to the barber and give him a thruppenny tip. He would take it solemnly, and say, 'Thank you, Master Kevin.' I was ten.

In my third year I was selected to play for Christ the King First XI soccer team. Dad took me to a sports shop on Belvoir Street, opposite the hairdresser's, to buy my first pair of football boots. He insisted I get a pair of the new 'continental' design and they later caused a sensation in the school changing-rooms: the other boys had boots that were more suitable for wearing down a coal mine. I was so proud. What a superb father to have! The Christ the King First XI consisted of ten boys of Irish origin and a Polish goalkeeper. A fat Polish goalkeeper. Needless to say, we played eleven, won eleven. I assumed this was because we were basically Irish. In my mind it was axiomatic. Irish was best.

Yet I was a quintessential English schoolboy, wholly jingoistic and totally preoccupied with sport and war. Dad indulged me in these preoccupations, letting me to stay up and watch the television series *Victory at Sea* and *War in the Air*. I would sit curled up beside him in his armchair, drinking hot Bovril, and thrilling at the sight of burning cities and sinking ships. He took me to see the epic British war films *Reach for the Sky*, *Above Us the Waves*, *The Cockleshell Heroes* and of course, *The Dam Busters*, one of the most brilliant war films ever made, and, I now recognize, one of the more perniciously mendacious. But back then I hero-worshipped the leader of the raid, Guy Gibson, who, I knew, was killed later in the war. I made up a song in his honour, to the tune of the 'Dambusters March'. I would emotionally sing, 'Guy Gibson fought and died,' after which I ran out of words. Oscar Hammerstein had little reason to fear me.

So Dad absolutely did not conform to the Irish Catholic stereotype. He was an ardent Tory, detested the National Health Service, disliked state interference in anything, and was right-wing on almost all social and political issues. On his bedside table were British military medals won by an ancestor in some nineteenth-century war. He taught me to sing 'British Grenadiers', marching on the spot beside the fireplace in the sitting room. When in October 1956 the BBC announced that RAF bombers had attacked Egyptian bases, my mother cried out, horrified, 'Oh my God.' But Dad's face was hard and set. 'That'll teach them.' Well, I agreed with Dad. War was thrilling! It was brilliant! Dad was not merely serious about supporting the war, and not just pro British, but he was keenly pro Empire. Today I regard the British attack on Suez, by the standards established at Nuremberg, to be a war crime. The moral basis was not dissimilar to those for which men were hanged after the Second World War: the assertion by violence of one state over a weaker state. But back then, I thought it was so exciting, because I knew so much about the weapons involved. The previous Christmas my parents had given me *The Eagle Book of Aircraft*, which in my considered opinion was, and probably still is, the finest book ever published. With Suez, I avidly watched the television news and read the newspapers for reports of the aircraft types I knew: the English Electric Canberra, the Vickers Valiant, the De Havilland Sea Venom and the Hawker Sea Hawk. Even now, those words Hawker Sea Hawk embody all the swashbuckling, seafaring myths of England, which I had imbibed with an indiscriminate gusto.

However, for sheer beauty, no aeroplane compared with the four-engine Handley Page Victor B1, which I once saw slowly flying low over Christ the King. It was painted a brilliant anti-nuclear flash white, and it shone like an ice cap against the bright opalescence of that blue midwinter sky. The Victor was like a vast, elegantly winged whale. It had crescent wings, and its pointed nose swelled out in a curved bulge to house both the bomb bay and the crew compartment, before tapering along its fuselage towards its swept-back cetaceous T-shaped tail. I have seen the 'Mona Lisa' and the 'Pieta' and that masterpiece of Impressionism, Renoir's 'Bal au Moulin de la Galette', and frankly, I think the Victor (on that day anyway) is superior to the lot.

On the morning of 11 March 1956 Mum burst into my bedroom – yes, burst – with the morning paper in her hand. A British pilot, Lt Commander Peter Twiss DSC, had just broken the world air-speed record in a Fairey Delta II, flying at 1132 mph. I was right all along! I ran into the bathroom, where Dad was shaving, to tell him the thrilling news. That morning was one of the happiest of my childhood. Soon the skies were going to full of wonderful British aircraft, better than anything the Americans could make.

Well, the Fairey Delta II was an experimental dead end. Moreover, my much loved Handley Page Victor was no more than a flying coffin that would have trouble surviving a Guy Fawkes missile from the independent and sovereign state of Myètopia, never mind Soviet air defences. Only two of the five crew had ejector seats; the rest had to bail out of a side door, directly in front of the engine intakes that would instantly have turned them into roseate vapour trails: three thoroughly British deaths. The technology that gave me so much childish pleasure (and for which I am so very grateful) was in fact a monumental British folly, almost laid on for my childhood pleasure. Never has so much been spent by so many for just one.

I was a boys' boy, and therefore, my father's boy, a lad who also went trainspotting (I once saw the famous Blue Mallard, the Handley Page Victor of the railway track: a thing of astonishing beauty, it was, absurdly, steam powered). And, of course, I loved cars, solemnly advising Dad on what kind we should buy. Shortly after Christmas Dad suggested we – just the pair of us, as a treat – take a trip to town. It was, again, bitterly cold, and we went to Edgar Backus's bookshop, where he bought me a Biggles book, *Spitfires on Parade*, which he signed and dated with his fountain pen in the shop, and which I still have. By ill chance, both my shoes were holed, and my feet froze as we walked around town. But I really didn't care about these ice-cold feet. I was with my dad, just he and I, on a very special day.

For all my considerable but largely theoretical interest in girls' bodies, I knew nothing whatever about sex, and had no idea that 'fuck' actually had a meaning. But football was to change all that. One Wednesday afternoon, three of us footballers were walking down Glenfield Road after practice, our boots hanging by their laces from our hands, when one of my companions said, 'Ey up. 'ave you 'eard? Mick Kelly's fúcked Elizabeth McGowan.'

'Oo ya beauty,' gasped the other boy. ''e never did.'

'Fucked? What does "fucked her" mean?' I asked.

'It means 'e put his cock inside 'er cúnt.'

This was easily the most atrocious, unbelievable, revolting thing that I had ever heard. How could anything fit into a girl's bladder, and why would you even want it to? My companions largely agreed: we all three of us stopped dead in our tracks, bent forward and pretended to get sick, while our boots danced circles of indignant incredulity.

A larger shock awaited me. One Friday Kevin Mansfield was late for Mass. I waited with increasing anguish until it became terrifyingly clear that I was to be the lone server. But I didn't have an idea what to do. I'd learnt none of the procedures, because he would always whisper over the necessary instructions. So, unassisted, I had to prepare the altar, get the cruets for the wine, collect the hosts, lay out the priest's clothing, prepare the communion plate, and give the Pope a bath, for all I knew. Then I would have to dance in detailed attendance throughout the Mass, waiting upon the priest and giving the correct Latin responses, before a silent but zealously attentive congregation of some 360 pupils, twenty staff, many parents and of course, Ghengis Khan herself, Miss Bratt.

I nervously laid out the priest's vestments, and waited upon Canon Milligan as he robed. But of course I had laid them out in the wrong order, and I fled as the priest pointedly rearranged them. I next had to put the cruets of the water and wine in the sanctuary, but where? I plonked them down near the altar. I had to mark the gospel, but which one? Time raced by. My little stomach was heaving with terror. Then the moment of Mass arrived. I went out alone with Canon Milligan. There wasn't even a liturgy card from which to read the responses, Kevin never needing one, everything necessary being retained within that infuriatingly clever red-haired brain of his.

Well, the wonder was that I wasn't struck by the lightning of God's wrath, as I tottered the wrong way around the altar, bawling random responses to Canon Milligan's despairing Latin, and trying to give the poor bastard wine when he wanted water, and communion wafers when he wanted the gospels. When he rose to make his sermon, in my panic, I misinterpreted this as the end of the Mass, and left the hall completely. Seeing that he didn't follow me I then abjectly had to slink back in. Matters proceeded to get worse as I commandeered the priest's words and announced in Latin to Canon Milligan that I was forgiving him his sins. He cut across my babble by shouting 'Kyrie eleison' to which the reply should be the recititave 'Kyrie eleison', meaning 'Lord have mercy', but I replied 'Et cum spiritu tuo', meaning 'And with you.' At which point Canon Milligan told me, loudly, in English to shut up, and he would look after everything.

The Mass is usually an ecclesiastical recreation of the Last Supper, but this very special service was in fact Calvary Mark II, and centre stage, right there hanging on the middle cross with a nice long spear in his side, ladies and gentlemen, I give you Master Kevin Myers, the boy with the nice middle-class fringe and a thruppeny tip in his paw.

The word does not exist to convey the sheer venom of the silence that emanated from Canon Milligan as I later attempted to help him disrobe. Worse was to come. Miss Bratt later came to my class to berate me in public: yes, finally, the sponge of vinegar. I was never to serve Mass at Christ the King again, she declared, and by Christ the King I never did. It took me many years to realize why Canon Milligan had not savagely rebuked me after Mass was finished, for this this gamey old celibate actually had three children by his equally gamey young housekeeper, a secret known only to one man in the parish, who never whispered a word to anyone, his GP, Dr W.G. Myers (FRCSI).

Six

ONE DAY, rummaging around in a metal box in the attic, I found a dented fireman's helmet. I took it down and asked Mum what it was. 'Your great uncle Jack's helmet from the Dublin Fire Brigade.' Uncle Jack was the man who had effectively raised Dad as his own son, and this was therefore a precious family heirloom – yet I was allowed to play with it. I put it on Johnny, and then threw rocks at it to to how resilient they both were: Johnny, as it turned out, the more so. In time I completely destroyed the helmet, but Dad didn't seem to care. Indeed, his childhood appeared to be someone else's, about which he seldom talked apart from the odd routine curse upon the brows of the Christian Bothers.

But he did tell me some of tales of Irish prowess serving with the British army on the battlefields in his youth. He proudly describing the landings of the Royal Dublin Fusiliers in Gallipoli in 1915. The landing point (V Beach, as I was later to learn) was enclosed by two spits of land reaching out on either side, so making it both a small bay and a death trap, with the Irish troops being fired on from three sides as they foundered offshore in their rowing boats.

'There was a British naval flier called Samson who flew over the bay, and when he landed, he said the entire bay was red,' he told me. 'That was Irish blood, by Jove, and I can tell you this – Irish soldiers are the bravest of any soldiers anywhere in the world.'

I particularly remember the name of Lt Commander Samson, because at school we had just been learning about another gentleman of that name, and his helpmeet Delilah, and in the way of the childish mind I'd wondered if the two men were somehow mysteriously related. Dad, who generally despised the clergy, spoke highly of just one priest: Father Willie Doyle. This Irish chaplain with the Royal Dublin Fusiliers had been a legend on the Western Front, bringing succour to injured soldiers, no matter their religion, until he inevitably met his end in the mud of Flanders.

Around the time that the British empire reasserted itself with its criminal attack on Suez, the IRA performed a comparably melancholy journey back in time with a fresh campaign in Northern Ireland. My father was incandescent with fury. 'They're murderers,' he told me (aged nine and three-quarters). 'A bunch of murderers and blackguards. That's all they are. Murderers and blackguards.'

'Blackguards' – that was the worst word that I ever heard my father use. He told me of the IRA bombings in Coventry in 1939, and of the young girl who was blown to pieces while she was out shopping for her wedding day. Needless to say, I had never previously heard of the IRA, or the Black and Tans, the special police the British had introduced to Ireland in 1920 to cope with the rising tide of IRA violence. He told me that he and another young man were walking down a Dublin street and the Black and Tans opened fire on them from a Crossley tender (I'd never heard that term before, either). He had managed to take cover, but his friend didn't, and – I think – died from his injuries. But it seemed that both the Black and Tans and the IRA were bad. How could both sides be bad in a war? Didn't there have to be a good side and a bad side, in all wars?

These stories did not form part of a childhood narrative, but were merely isolated rocks being dropped into that largely rock-less pool of my mind. I can place context and continuity on them now, but not then, for only in adulthood do the brain's synapses finally connect the separate shoals of memory, ego and appetite, which together make up the mental archipelago of any individual.

One afternoon, the following spring, Dad called the three Little Ones together. The wireless wasn't working, he said sternly. Had anyone been interfering with it? We solemnly shook our heads.

'I see. We'd better investigate.' He lifted the huge wooden cabinet out of the cavity in the wall, put it on the table, and opened up the back. 'By Jove, what have we got here?' he whispered in awe. Like a magician amazed by his own genius, he produced a huge wad of five- and ten-pound notes.

I raced into the kitchen.

'Quickly, quickly, Mum,' I cried, 'you've got to see this.' I dragged her into the sitting room, where Dad was laying out hundreds of pounds in notes on the table. 'How much is there, Dad?'

'Six hundred pounds at least!' he cried. 'Someone must have hidden this here, years and years ago. And now it's ours. A miracle! No worries for this family from now on,' and he rubbed his hands with glee.

'Look, Mum, a miracle, a fortune, and out of nowhere!' A look half of worry, half of impatience, sat on Mum's face. She turned and left, while Dad, chortling, recounted the money. Even now, I don't know what he was up to, or why he had taken all this money out of the bank and hidden it in the radio, but a strange behavioural pattern was emerging

One night I was woken by loud angry shouts from downstairs. Maggy crept into my room in fear, and slipped into bed beside me. We both lay there, paralyzed.

'My heart, my poor heart,' I heard Dad whimper.

'I am sick and bloody tired of your poor heart,' cried Mum. 'I don't give a damn about your bloody heart anymore.'

This language was shocking. My mother never used words like that. Further shouting and screaming followed. I could hear Ann's voice in the verbal maelstrom. Later, I heard the voice of Zbishik Ludwig, Dad's Polish partner, whom presumably Ann had called, and who had come over to calm things down. She stole into the bedroom and told us there had been a row, but all was well, and we should forget everything. But that was impossible. What was this about my father's heart? And was Mum mocking him or scolding him over it? I sided emphatically with poor Dad.

A shadow had fallen on family life. Over the coming days Dad took to staying in bed, initially for hours, then not leaving it at all. He would start weeping, and his cries would fill the house. To my mind, this was unmanly: this was disgusting.

Some weeks later, Mum asked me to go up and see Dad.

'But Mum. All that sobbing and stuff. It's horrible.'

'He's not well. Just go up, please, will you?'

'All right.'

'Don't tell him I sent you.'

Dad lay in bed, the contours of his face quite broken, as if the skin around his eyes had been burned and etched with acid.

'Hello, Dad.'

He sobbed. I stood there, saying nothing, while he wept. 'Why are you here?' he finally asked. I said nothing. 'It was because your mother told you to come up, wasn't it?' I stayed silent. 'Wasn't it?'

'Yes.' He began weeping again. I left, my heart sick with contempt.

'How is he?' asked my mother.

'Crying again.'

'You didn't tell him I told you to go up, did you?'

'Yes.'

'But I told you not to!'

'He asked me.'

Dad was sent away for treatment in Newcastle. I resumed my life, as children do, adapting to the new normalities rather like water uncomplainingly follows the lie of the land it is flooding. I certainly didn't think about the future, a tense that has no generalized meaning for children.

The following summer we rented a couple of chalets in Cornwall, a ridiculously long way from Leicester. We arrived after nightfall and Mum opened some tinned stew while us children sliced string beans in the kitchen and watched the rainwater trickle down the windows. Dinner was vile. So was the weather next morning, and every day thereafter, for two weeks, while Dad stayed in bed, weeping. A nearby chalet was occupied by the Braithwaites, who, just like Michael Parker years before, reminded me how un-English we really were. The Braithwaites were neat and orderly, polite and predictable. Mrs Braithwaite led them all in twee and infuriating little sing-songs during mealtimes, such as 'Daddy Long Legs Are We'. The Braithwaites always got to the communal showers first thing in the morning, and the hot water was all gone by the time we arrived. They weren't being selfish – it was just that in those days England regarded hot water as being rather like myrrh.

Later, hearing these little English children singing their bloody little heads off over breakfast, with my Irish Dad making a fool of himself, lying in bed all day, weeping, I was torn. On the one hand, I yearned to take an axe and slay these warbling little fucking Braithwaites, but on the other hand, I really wanted to be like them.

Dad called me to see him on the last day there, and asked if I had enjoyed the holiday. No, I said. Why not? he asked.

'It was just horrible,' I said. 'Why can't we be like the Braithwaites, and happy?'

He wept again, and I left.

FEW PEOPLE have the willpower and the wherewithal to be what they actually want in life. Most of us are borne on tides of others' making, steered by circumstance, carried on the current of our own inertia, and blown by the unrelenting sea breeze of weakness. The daily struggle is the long lap to sunset without succumbing to the quotidian. And that is sufficiently confusing without waves of chronic illness commandeering a family's life. That we children all got through the confused and terrible days and years that were to follow speaks volumes for the love and the zeal of the mother who raised us. Norah Myers was a loving, cheerful and wonderful homemaker, just as she was also the guardian of our social status. It was she who decided that the boys should go to boarding school, and Ann to Loreto Convent in St Alban's. Through sickness and health she made afternoon tea every day throughout the school holidays, a formal meal of cakes and scones. She herself had been educated at Loreto, which put manners on the young ladies of England, and also one of Ireland, and she knew about the crushing social decorum of middle-class English life.

When she moved to Devon she already knew what was expected of her. A lady newcomer must not ask a local making her first visit to take off her coat, or invite her into the sitting room, but merely to take her calling card. She would return the call, but to accept any comparable invitation (laid as carefully as honey in a bear trap) was to invite certain and permanent social exclusion thenceforth. Instead, she would leave her card, and a delicate minuet of social ice-breaking would follow over the coming days: oh I don't know, maybe one glove would come off for the third visit, both gloves the next, the coat the one after, and the hat for the following one and maybe on the fifteenth day, the girls would all settle down to an orgy of English nudity and some good old lesbian sex. Or perhaps not.

Most social mores produce a tyranny of some kind, as I was soon to discover. Children at Christ the King intending to take communion at the weekly Mass on Fridays would sit at the very front of the school hall. One morning as I left the kitchen bound for school, I dipped my finger in the sugar bowl and licked it. As usual, I took my place at the front of the hall. It was only as other children rose to take communion that I realized that by licking the sugar, I had broken my fast. If, having eaten, one took communion, it was a violation of the Holy Sacrament, and not merely a sin but a mortal sin, for which one would certainly go to hell. This hell was not a metaphor, but a real place of fire and teeth-gnashing torment, where I would spend the rest of eternity

What could I do? I couldn't just stay kneeling there all alone, the one sinner from a line of perfect children. So I rose with them and shuffled on to kneel at the altar rail as Canon Milligan approached. Then, with Kevin Mansfield holding the silver patten beneath my chin, I finally put out my tongue and received and swallowed the body of Jesus Christ Almighty. At that moment, I became a mortal sinner. As I returned to my seat, my brain was thundering with terror and guilt and a vertiginous and unmitigated horror. I was doomed, doomed, doomed. The everlasting torment of hell awaited me.

Each Saturday for three years, I had gone to confession at St Peter's Church, with almost nothing to confess. Indeed, I regularly confessed to some invented sins in order to give the poor devil before me something to absolve. Yet now I was the custodian of the worst sin in the history of St Peter's parish. The following Saturday I rattled through the usual confabulation of trite misdemeanours and tried to summon up the courage to confess the Big One. But my nerve failed. Yet to withhold a mortal sin during confession was itself another and very special kind of mortal sin, a reserved sin that could only be forgiven by a bishop.

The next day at family Mass I could not defect from the line of Myerses piously queuing to receive communion, so I took it again, compounding the evil I had already done. That I was sooner or later bound for the inferno of everlasting damnation, I did not doubt. Sometimes in the coming weeks of torment, I managed to lock up my terror in a small part of my brain, and keep it there. But at night, I would often lie awake, tormented by the weight of my crimes.

Mostly I lived the usual outdoor life of a healthy boy. Other boys in the area went around on little carts that their father had made for them. We Myerses didn't, because everyone knew that it couldn't be expected of a doctor. Having seen his car jack and his dry flies in action, I wasn't especially sorry. Tragically, we didn't have a sledge when the snows came, as they did every winter, and the children of the neighbourhood would make for a nearby hill, The Buttercup Fields. The girls wore skirts, the boys, shorts. Almost no one wore jeans and our knees were chapped and bleeding after being scraped for hour upon hour through the ice. That didn't worry me as much as having to borrow Mark's sledge, which was almost as unseemly as borrowing someone's mother.

Moreover, I was now old enough to venture to The Sand Hills half a mile away. These 'hills' consisted of a raised mile-wide plateau of clay, with the far side of the plain ending in a series of hedged gullies and ravines. It was an untouched wilderness, around which Leicester had developed. Vagrant, mystical diddicoy came here in their caravans and their herds of painted horses, like the last descendants of an ancient Asian horde. In one secret corner of The Sand Hills, gamblers from nearby estates gathered in a well-worn circle to play pitch and toss, with lookouts posted to warn of the police. This was where I really began to understand some of the many differences between the sexes. I was outlining my game to a group of children. Half our gang was to be Japanese and German, an SS Bushido unit (I had enthusiastically read Lord Russell's *Scourge of the Swastika* and *Knights of the Bushido*) and the other half – my half – was to be British commandos. We would bayonet all the other lot, and take no prisoners. A girl called Nora spoke up. 'Can I be a nurse, please?' I vetoed that revolting idea with a manly shudder, and with the outfit divided into two, we started our game. It was a warm work, and soon I had killed many, many Germans and Japanese. But when I turned to review my path of slaughter, to my horror, I beheld Nora, kneeling beside a body of a Japanese SS man whom

I had, only moments before, rather fabulously disembowelled. 'What are you doing?' I cried, appalled.

'Taking his temperature,' she sighed. 'We might just save him.'

Wild little working-class girls from the nearby Stocking Farm Estate, slightly older than me, used to play with uninhibited gusto on The Sand Hills. They seemed so deliciously and fascinatingly wanton: occasionally, a girl might even stop mid game to haul down her knickers to pee without apology or explanation. Older Sand Hill girls flirted with boys, though not of course with me, and sometimes, they even kissed them. They were exotic and raw and, yes, they had The Knowledge. I didn't know what The Knowledge was, but they knew. Even though I was only ten, sex was in the air. These pre-adolescent yearnings caused a faintly pleasurable nausea in the pit of the stomach, and a yearning for something indefinable. It was nuanced and gentle and almost nostalgic, a puzzled and puzzling sensuality in what was unquestionably a child's body.

I used to daydream of finding one my classmates, Catherine Carey, alone and completely naked on The Sand Hills, and in my fantasy, I would instantly take off my school blazer to conceal her nakedness. She would kiss me in chaste gratitude: that was that, the beginning and unaroused end of it. I told Mark about this, and yes, he too would daydream of a certain girl named Patricia Greenwood whom he would find naked and would then protect, and she would reward him also with a Cinderella kiss.

At school, I sat in the back row of class near another Patricia, surname Lord. She was a freckled redhead with unwavering brown eyes. Sometimes, while we were meant to be doing an exercise and the teacher was marking other classwork, she would go into a strange kind of oblivion. Her face would droop down close to the desk, and she would breathe heavily. She wasn't writing. One evening she caught up with me as I left school and asked if she could walk with me. She invited me into her house. Her parents were not in. She took me through the kitchen and half pushed me into the outside toilet. Her mood was strangely urgent, and she frightened me – girls didn't scare boys, it's the other way round. I had no idea what she wanted. She became more forcible. I pushed my way out of the little cubicle and ran home.

A couple of days later, I caught her cheating in an exam and publicly denounced her to the teacher. A palpable shock passed through the class at such an act of treachery. The teacher gently rebuked Patricia but scolded me roundly for telling tales. Peter Keegan, he who had crushed Dermot Browne, came up to me after class and hit me. He was right, of course, and I knew it. But I didn't act out of malice so much as a confused fear. Patricia was different. I wanted her punished, excluded. Only in very recent years have I learnt that Patricia's behaviour – the obsessive public masturbation, the precocious and uncontrolled libido – are clear signs of childhood abuse. And though most of the silly wrongs we do in childhood vanish from our minds, my betrayal of poor Patricia Lord lies on my conscience yet.

The invisible police of our souls was provided by St Peter's Church, and its chief constable was Canon Milligan, that formidable old liar and rascal. A succession of priests, most of them Irish, came as his accomplices. Of his curates, quite the most tragic was Father Ignatius Forde, whom God had graced with almost every kind of impediment. His cheekbones stuck out like knitting-needle points from an almost fleshless face. He was nearly blind, and deep behind his spectacles, a brace of minuscule pupils darted in perpetual terror, like those of a small hunted mammal in a cave. Above a narrow ridge of forehead sat tightly wound coils of greasy hair, which showered an indiscriminate blizzard of dandruff upon his cassocked shoulders. He had huge tombstone teeth, which formed an apex at his incisors. Whenever he ate a sandwich on one of his many, many pastoral visits to the Myers home, each mouthful left a small triangular incision. But his real triumph was a stutter so disabling for a priest that it was like a man with frostbitten hands embarking on a career as a card sharp. The opening incantation of the old Mass ran, '*In nomina Patris, et Fili, and Spiritus Sancti. Amen. Introibo ad altare Deum.*' He would open his mouth to say the initial 'In'. Then nothing. Absolutely nothing, save a sickened, expectant silence across the church, while his triangular upper incisors bit lumps out of the air and gobbets of saliva flew like a cobra trying to shoot down dancing flies. Then he would stop, inhale deeply, and open his mouth again, as the altar boys began to pray for divine intervention. The congregation would silently urge the Virgin Mary to help. The choir possibly even began negotiations with the devil to compel him to speak. Dr Myers was rattling his keys, while Mrs Myers and her entire brood were almost shrieking aloud. But no sound emerged, as his jaws bit off lumps of air.

Finally, for no obvious reason, the dam wall would finally burst, and the rest of the liturgy would come blurting out in a torrent of spittle and misplaced consonants. Then came the time for Father Forde to head for the pulpit, when the entire church would freeze. Vast throngs of despairing prayers would depart heavenwards: Dear Sweet Jesus, get him through this. Please, dear God, for the love of your Divine Mother, no more pauses, no more silences, no more yawning verbal vacuums, and most of all, sweet and kind and ever-loving Jesus, no more fucking spit. But then spit was what we would almost long for, as poor Forde's teeth snatched at empty air in his desperate quest to begin his sermon, his maimed, nail-less fingers frantically roaming over the pulpit stonework, like a blind hotel guest who smells smoke and is frantically scanning the manager's cheery welcome in Braille, looking for the fire drill.

Yet Father Forde was an object of universal pity, not scorn, for Christian charity was an authentic part of the culture of that community of St Peter's. Christian tolerance coexisted with the toxically irrational guilt of the kind besetting my soul. This is not uniquely Catholic, but human nature: opposing streams occupying the same riverbed, each certain of the path it is following, but seemingly unaware of the integral immanence of an entirely contradictory moral order. How else does the well-nourished Christian eat when the hungry are within eyesight? You can call it hypocrisy, but in reality, it is merely a coping technique – for the alternative, of seeking perfect consistency in such a profoundly inconsistent world, is probably one sure road to madness.

Central to our Catholic faith was a doctrine of charity that was both real and lived. We had to be courteous to everyone, and Dad insisted that old Mr Campbell in particular was deserving of a special respect. Whenever he passed we were to stop playing and politely bid him the time of day. Mr Campbell was Irish, a retired policeman, and his once-mighty frame was now stooped and his gait slow. He always wore a black overcoat and a black homburg, and on Sunday mornings would make his way with stately infirmity to the nearby Blackbird pub. On his return homeward, if we were playing in the front garden – and we usually made it our business to be – he would give us sixpence to divide between us. Mr Campbell's tanner was nearly the high point of a Sunday in non-conformist Leicester. Even the swings in the nearby Abbey Park were chained on the Sabbath to prevent us wicked children enjoying ourselves. For different versions of sin prevailed in different versions of the Christianity of my childhood, and in what better place than in Abbey Park? For Cardinal Wolsey had died here during his dispute with Henry VIII.

The historically interesting parts of Leicester were within walking distance of Medina Road, so we always had places to show visitors from Ireland, which is how Johnny and I took Mum's older brother Tom Teevan, a High Court judge in Dublin, to the ruins in Abbey Park.

'This is where Cardinal Wolsey died,' declared Johnny proudly, though I think neither one of us actually knew who Wolsey was.

'Poor Cardinal Wolsey died here, did he? In that case, we'll say a decade of the rosary for the repose of his immortal soul.'

'What?' I said incredulously. 'You mean, here?'

'Naturally. Sure isn't this where the poor man died?'

'But Uncle Tom, he's been dead centuries.'

'There's no such thing as centuries in the hereafter,' said Tom, as he laboriously got down on his knees, and took out his rosary beads.

'But Uncle Tom … everyone will see us!'

'And why shouldn't they see us? Sure, they're going to hear us, aren't they?'

'What? Oh, Uncle Tom, we're not really going to pray out loud, are we?'

'Certainly we are. Now kneel down, if you please.'

Johnny and I exchanged looks of wan horror before slinking down, almost on all fours, as if looking for a sixpence lost in the grass.

'Our Father, who art in Heaven, hallowed be thy name,' clarioned Tom at the top of his voice, as passers-by began to slow, stop and stare. Just about everyone I knew came to Abbey Park, including the Woodgate Mau Maus and the Gene Drive cannibal gang, never mind the Apaches from The Sand Hills with their sultry, knickerless molls. And now, dear God, I might well be found on my knees and praying aloud by any or all of these savages.

'But … but … but …' I protested.

'Hail Mary full of grace,' bawled Uncle Tom. Thus Johnny and I raced through our response for the ten Hail Marys like a group of Alabama auctioneers in a slave sale amid rumours of an imminent uprising amongst the merchandise. The decade ended with a Glory Be; glory be indeed, the horror was now over, with my public piousness still unseen. I was beginning to rise, when Tom warbled: 'The second decade. Our Father, who art in Heaven …'

I haggardly scanned the horizon for the local Sioux and Arapahoe, all too aware of the scalping ahead if I were observed actually praying in public. We got through twenty whole Hail Marys, plus a roster of Our Fathers and Glory Be's, before Tom finally and slowly rose. He looked sadly around at the ruins before adding: 'I suppose it was Henry VIII who did for this place.'

'Are we going to pray for him too, now?' whimpered an incredulous Johnny.

'Indeed we are not, the infidel.'

The discovery of Richard III's bones in 2012 in Friary Lane has revolutionized Leicester's attitude to its history – but in my childhood, most local folk seemed utterly indifferent to it. Indeed, forgetting their history almost completely seems to be as characteristic of the English as getting theirs almost completely wrong is a characteristic of the Irish.

The park was just beyond Blackbird Road, where an early industrial dispute in a bakery concerning a pay increase and the adulteration of bread with non-wheat grains had given the English-speaking world the nursery rhyme, 'Sing a song of sixpence, a pocket full of rye, four and twenty blackbirds, baked in a pie'. And St Peter's Church was beside The Blue Boar Inn, where Richard III had supposedly slept the night before he led his Yorkist cause to a common ruin at Bosworth Field in 1483. Mark's uncle Jack Chumley (also uncle of Pip) once told me that he had been clearing soil near Market Bosworth and it was full of human bones.

'But they must be the dead of the Battle of Bosworth Field,' I cried excitedly. 'Boswor' wha'?' glowered Jack, his toothless gums gnawing on a piece of tea-soaked bread. I explained the battle, and how Henry VII had come onto the throne because of it.

'Oo ah? Well bones are in rubbish dump now,' he cackled mordantly. He'd lost all his teeth in a Japanese POW camp, so I dare say more recent deaths weighed more heavily upon him than those of Bosworth Field.

Granny was a regular visitor, with a terrifying grasp of genealogies. Once we went to collect her at the bus station after she had been visiting Aunt Enid in Blackpool. Despite her considerable age and infirmity she was first off the bus and introduced us to every single passenger as they alighted: in the course of the journey she had interrogated each one of them to within an inch of their now shattered lives, to establish any possible molecules of Irish ancestry.

'This is Mr Blenkinsop from Derby, who is visiting his cousin. His maternal grandmother was an O'Malley from Mayo, but he thinks his father's grandmother might have come from Carlow. He's promised to stay in touch.'

A quivering Mr Blenkinsop would pass by on all fours before making a palsied bid for freedom, while Granny introduced us to the next passenger.

'And this is Mrs Fosdyke! Her mother was a Sweeney from Donegal, not one of the Letterkenny Sweeneys, but the Inishowen Sweeneys. I was at school with her third cousin once removed, Maureen, a lovely girl – if a little plump – who joined the Little Sisters of the Holy Child, and became a missionary, and was eaten by South Sea Islanders. I did warn her, but did she listen? And quite remarkably, Mr Fosdyke's cousin Beryl on his father's side is married to Seamus Doherty from Dungloe, the better Dohertys, the ones with the drapery shop, not the publican Dohertys, nice enough in their own way. Seamus The Draper Doherty's mother was a Gallagher, and a great-great-grand-niece of my great-uncle Charlie, because his granddad had married his own great-aunt, who also happened to be his sister.'

A twitching Mrs Fosdyke would be taken away on a stretcher as the others, whey-faced and trembling, passed through the final valley of death after enduring the bus journey from hell in the company of Annie Teevan, born Annie O'Brien of Strabane.

I have already introduced her daughter, the delightful Aunt Enid. The Little Ones once accompanied Mum to greet her at London Road railway station, and almost by divine command, her compartment stopped at precisely where we were standing on the platform. She was gazing imperiously out of the window, her matted wig at a jaunty angle and her dentures bared in disdainful, lipstick-stained greeting. Behind her sat five wide-eyed West Indians and Indians.

'Thank God – some white faces at last,' she declared. 'I've been surrounded by niggers ever since Manchester.'

Far from being indignant, her fellow passengers bore looks of almost ecstatic relief. They knew their torment was now ending, whereas ours, as they rightly guessed, was just beginning.

ENID SAT watching me finishing my lamb chop. 'Lamb chops, as you know, Willie, are the most potent source of threadworm,' she said, speaking across me to Dad. 'Did you know that, you?' she added, addressing me.

'Please, Aunt Enid, what are threadworm?'

'Threadworm infest the faeces of little boys like you, if they're dirty, and they can emerge from the anus at night and migrate into the anus of someone sleeping nearby. Did you ever get threadworm? You might have given them to someone else. You certainly have the unhealthy look of a child riddled with threadworm.'

My father would clear his throat and glare with those dark eyes at such cruel thrusts, but he didn't quite have the strength of personality to rebuke Enid, as he should really have done, with an iron shovel over her brains and a secret burial at midnight.

Once she took me aside and said, 'Has anyone ever told you that you have a squint? You should be wearing spectacles to correct it, otherwise you could go blind. Of course if you have been abusing yourself, it's probably too late. You're the sort of horrid boy who would be. Tell me. Have you been abusing yourself?'

'No Aunt Enid,' I replied, with no idea of what 'abusing yourself' meant. The next day I was in the dining-room singing the sea shanty 'The Rio Grande' when Enid came in and shushed me. 'Ah, as I suspected, you're tone deaf! How extraordinary. Totally flat – yet you clearly think that you're singing in tune. Are you sure you haven't been abusing yourself?'

'No, Aunt Enid. I mean, yes, Aunt Enid.'

'Hmm. Very well. Please do not sing in my hearing again.'

Seven

THE WORLD that I grew up in evolved almost as if to accommodate me and my generation. I see the old photographs of Medina Road and the very young Myers children: these capture the bleak austerity and greyness of adult life at the time, a rationed, monotone regimen of indigenous starches and muddy root vegetables supplemented by tinned meats from Argentina and Nebraska. The arrival of BBC television as I reached the cusp of awareness and boredom was a thoughtful deed by a kindly providence. Just as I might have grown tired of the BBC's patrician complacency, Independent Television lurched in like a drunken prole, kissing the bride at a royal wedding.

I loved the vulgarity and tastelessness on ITV, the common touch for the common person. My favourite TV advertising jingle was the immortal 'You'll wonder where the yellow went, when you brush your teeth with Pepsodent'. People probably did have yellow teeth when smoking was almost universal. The morning bus queue always left a variegated spoor of clotted phlegm on the kerbside, as commuters deep-inhaled their first cigarette of the day, and coughed up some of the rich bronchial residue from the day before, while other residues lingered to perform some lethal alchemy within. I would gaze enviously at the multicoloured glue of these pavement deposits, and think that when I grew up I, too, might generate such rich adult beauty.

And almost overnight, as the last of the rationing vanished, our lives were filled with new and exciting consumer goods. There was Dab-It-Off, a stain remover that replaced the original smaller blemish with a far wider and now permanent one; Chocolate Ex-Lax to cater to the British national obsession with unmoved bowels; British Dinky toys, whose wheels always wobbled and jammed, and German toys, which always worked perfectly and lasted for ever. There was Tizer, awash with life-enhancing chemicals, and Amplex, the oral deodorizer, which killed bad breath as effectively as a dead mouse round the neck cures cancer. There were crazes like the hula hoops, which caused slipped discs, and Davy Crockett hats, which went out of favour the moment retailers had stocked up on them, causing a nationwide epidemic of bankruptcies. For the first time in history the children's market, dominated by my generation, could enrich or ruin you.

But the greatest cultural revolution occurred when I was about seven. Popular music up until this time largely conformed to the dance-time rules that reached from nineteenth-century music hall to the vaudeville, and the popular light tenors of the early 1950s, who largely remained true to the American antebellum ballad traditions of Stephen Foster. Then along came Bill Haley and Elvis Presley. Only those who had been bobbing gently in an ocean composed entirely of the turgid brine of crooners' love songs and winsome animal ditties can grasp the raw emotional impact of rock and roll as it happened. The first time I heard Elvis Presley's 'Hound Dog' it was as if someone had opened a shutter into my soul. It was exciting in ways that were subliminal and hormonal and dangerous and even dirty, hinting of far vaster things to come. The music of America poured across the Atlantic and changed the emotional world inhabited by everyone, but most of all, by the young.

Mark's brother Jim had bought a new record, 'Sixteen Tons', by Tennessee Ernie Ford, and one lunchtime, Mark and I played it over and over. It wasn't pure rock and roll, but it had a grittiness, a directness that reached deep within my young body. I had to go back to school, and as I left, I heard overhead the rare but unmistakable throbbing boom of Wright Cyclone piston engines – a USAF twin-engined Fairchild C 119D Packet troop transporter, flying low over 17 Medina Road. At that moment I felt a childish epiphany, as if the world were all one, and the entire episode of music plus aircraft had been mounted solely for me.

This exciting modern world co-existed alongside a very ancient and a very fierce world indeed. The Catholic sacrament of confirmation was an acceptance of the authority of the Church by a child rational enough to understand this. It can only be administered by a bishop, and all children must be without sin when receiving it. But I had licked sugar off my finger and then taken communion; this disqualified me from receiving confirmation, so I decided to confess. But when I arrived at the church, I found that the only priest hearing confessions that morning was Canon Milligan, whom – following the debacle of my solo run as an altar boy – I regarded with a special kind of terror. What would he make of such an admission? My nerve failed.

The next day, my entire class was confirmed. Child by child and cheek by cheek we went up to the altar and knelt, while Bishop Ellis passed along us, saying a few words, and tapping us each lightly on the face to warn us of the coming blows in life. For me, this cuff was no metaphor. I was taking a bishop-given sacrament in a state of mortal sin. Not merely was the sacrament invalid, and would therefore have to be repeated, but I had committed a 'reserved' sin, which could only be absolved by a bishop.

Meanwhile a succession of locums had been covering for Dad, who remained marooned on his tear-soaked island of chronic melancholia. Then he seemed to get better and started to take me to Filbert Street, the home of Leicester City Football Club, for which I soon developed a quite irresistible addiction. Time and distance allow me to see that it was all of a piece throughout: Dad, me, 17 Medina Road, Filbert Street, the football club and the city itself. This ascending order of incompetence resembled Russian dolls, small Babushkas of ineptitude.

Leicester – whose motto embodied its melancholy aspirations: *Semper Eadem*, Always the Same – was a city of little distinction that never got into the national news for anything, not even the shocking rocket attack on Titchley's chemist or the tragedy that was the Great Allotments Fire. Its football club was a reflection of general qualities. Mr Patterson said City (as we called it) deserved to be in a one-team league of its own, because it was neither good nor bad enough to play anyone else. For the most part its players, mostly local men, resembled bandy-legged bricklayers. Their hair was usually Brylcreemed into their scalps, and about half of them had false teeth, which they would remove before a game. Since Leicester folk usually watched the game in an unengaged silence, one of distinctive features of Filbert Street was the gummy babble of players calling for the ball.

Leicester's wingers trundled up and down the touch as if they were pushing wheelbarrows along tracks. Our defenders were clearly recruited from rude agrarian stock, as personified by our right back, Len 'Chopper' Chambers: any attacker who got close to him would be simply felled by a shin-high strike from the scythe that Chopper used instead of a foot. Without waiting for the whistle, he would instantly trot back a few paces and wait for the resulting free kick, while his stricken opponent scoured the grass looking for his missing limb. Our centre forward was a portly middle-aged man called Arthur Rowley, wittily dubbed Rowley-Poley. His technique was to stand ten feet from the goal line and tap the ball in. He seemed immune to the otherwise iron laws of offside.

Nonetheless, though Leicester players were as unfit as butchers' dogs, to my boyish mind they were sporting gods. Dad would take me through the all-ticket gate with him on his ticket, and assure the gatekeeper that I was little (as I was) and would spend the match on his knee. This was a little embarrassing, but I was only ten and didn't understand that the underlying issue wasn't cost: it was to give Dad company. He simply had no real friends. To be sure, he had many acquaintances of his own class, doctors like him, but they were not friends. Without me, he would have gone to those matches alone, watched them alone, and gone home alone.

I don't believe this singular singularity was caused by his melancholy. Some people are coated with a social Velcro that makes multiple friendships and others are born Velcro-free, no matter their decency, goodness and honesty. Poor Dad was apparently Velcro-free, for no one ever rang him to ask him out for a pint, or offered him a warm haven from the dark night that lay over his life. And so I was perforce Dad's friend, especially since my older brothers, Bill and David, were away at boarding school. Bill was already the great intellectual of the family, but at that time, a dedicated photographer with no interest in football. David, by his own choice, was bound for the priesthood, and similarly uninterested in football.

Their two hobbies provided much of the texture of the family. Most of the family photographic record came from Bill's camera, and he had improvised a darkroom under the stairs. Almost uniquely for a boy of his age, he developed and printed all his own film, and the hall duly reeked of mysterious, light-sensitive chemicals and the emulsions that turn their chemical memories into lasting images. David, meanwhile, loved animals, and single-handedly created the Myers menagerie. A tortoise (named Todd, after Mike Todd, the film director) was probably the least troublesome of his beasts, despite its domestic policy of leaving long grey faeces on the lawn precisely where we would sun ourselves on both days in the year when this was possible. Numerous stick insects and hamsters entered the home – the motionless mantises to leave their surprisingly large droppings on the breakfast table, and the hamsters to vanish into the interior plumbing of the range, where they joined the resident mice in a pioneering experiment in rodent multiculturalism. It didn't work, of course. One day, while sitting on the sofa, Granny felt some major event occurring beneath her bottom. She slowly stood and lifted the cushion to reveal field mice and hamsters engaged in a vast race riot, the sight of which propelled her portly, 82-year-old frame several feet into the air.

MARK CAME breathlessly to me one day. 'Ey oop, Kev! 'Ave y' 'eard? There were a kid wa go' rattacked by a blúddy great python on Roedean Crescent. Bi' ris arm off. Nearly blúddy swallowed 'im, only his dad go' ris 'eels and pulled 'im aht, júst in toim. We're putting together a posse to go look for i'. Are ya cúmmin'?'

We joined a couple of boys from Mark's school and equipped with sticks, went thwacking through the long grass of the lotties, desperately hoping to see one of our number vanishing any second. Mrs Patterson suddenly appeared, her jowls quivering with concern.

'Marcús! Marcús!' she cried: 'You cúm on on on in out on it, raht now, afore you get rúddy ett.' She ushered a mortified Mark away, while the rest of us deputies intrepidly continued our hunt. Soon afterwards a truant Mark reappeared, his pride restored. Susan Padstow came running up and said the snake had been seen on Brading Crescent, where it nearly killed an old-age pensioner. We raced there to find some white-faced women in a feverish gossip cluster.

'Did you see it?' we panted.

'Did ah see it? Blúddy 'ell, near took Mrs Arkwright's rúddy 'and off,' cried a woman with a knotted duster on her head. 'Rossers is coming. That'll sort vicious búgger out.'

The police duly arrive, armed with nets and poles and warrants for entering people's gardens. Mark and I were standing with Dad outside the house, revelling in the sheer African terror of it all.

'I want you to keep a sharp look-out, you two especially,' said the policeman, pointing at me and Mark. We nearly saluted him.

That evening Dad treated a number of women for shock, and emerged not a little exasperated at the general hysteria. 'Just as well your snake's under lock and key,' he said to David. My older brother's eyes glazed a little bit. 'It is locked up, isn't it?'

'Not quite. I took it for a walk yesterday. It got away. Sorry, Dad.' Only a Myers of Medina Road would take an eighteen-inch long serpent for a walk. However, its dimensional modesty did not prevent it becoming the rampaging anaconda of west Leicester, and by next morning Mark heard in school that several children had gone missing overnight. But we Myerses said nothing, and soon afterwards the giant snake vanished, along with all trace of the myth it had so dramatically if briefly inspired.

Dogs came our way too. There was a boxer, Jimmy James, with rather regrettable personal habits. One of Dad's patients had given it to us, perhaps in condign reparation for some premature bereavement. Jimmy James was named after a comedian with slobbering jowls, and for that very reason. His other primary characteristic was to rest his forepaws on my shoulders while he licked my face and encouraged me to do something with his huge red erection. At the time, I didn't really wonder about this strange protrusion from his belly, but since it was clear to my parents that Jimmy James and personal chastity would remain strangers, he and his gigantic lipstick were sent back whence they had come.

He was replaced by twin mongrel collies, Brutus and Caesar, who soon turned Dad's attempt at a garden into Flanders, circa 1917. So Dad erected a five-foot high metal cord running the length of the garden, to which he attached two chains on pulleys. The dogs could then run up and down a narrow strip of ruined garden, while the rest of it could revert to the semi-paradise that it had earlier been – namely, four roses, some docks, 200 dandelions, a hollyhock and a what-do-you-call-it. One night the two dog leads got entangled, and poor Caesar was throttled, leaving Brutus scampering backwards and forwards the length of the garden. With the arrival of spring, Maggy decided to take her bike from the garage and to cycle round the lawn – and with a delighted smile she rode directly into the wire, which smote across her face and sent her spiralling backwards from her bike seat.

Though Maggy, happily, was not seriously hurt, that little episode did it for Dad's dog run. The hawser was taken down and the back garden once again became safe for cycling. Inevitably Brutus escaped and was run over and killed. The Myers menagerie was now reduced to a single goldfish, but perhaps afflicted by the fatal miasma infusing Medina Road, this creature soon floated to the surface of its bowl, dead, and we duly wrapped it in cotton wool and buried it in the 'rose garden'. Two weeks later, anxious to see what a rotting fish looked like, we dug the corpse up. It was curiously un-decayed. I prodded it, and in reply, it wriggled. Johnny and I put it back in its fish bowl, and it survived for another six months, until we killed it with overfeeding.

Eight

DAD SOON RELAPSED, with fresh oceans of tears, fresh accessions of unspeakable unmanliness, and later that year, around November, he was admitted to the Isolation Hospital at the top of the Groby Road, a couple of miles away. Some nights later we went to visit him.

He lay silent in bed, not weeping, nor even complaining, probably as a result of electric-shock treatment. I hated every single second I was there. I hated the dull eyes, his old-man's flannel pyjamas, the strangely disconnected nurses who never saw you and talked around you, and the all-pervasive hospital smell of polish and stale urine and sweet excrement and fermenting sweat and thwarted disinfectant.

A milk pudding of a fog had fallen by the time we were driving home. Mum could see nothing, so we veered off the road and onto the kerb. I got out and led the way, feeling forward with my left hand, and holding onto the bonnet with my right. All around me in the suet-coloured smog, stranded motorists were calling for help, like voices echoing from Arctic floes. We, however, felt our way homeward, slowly but successfully, with me as a form of braille radar. And I wondered, as I led the way, and with the unreasonable reason of childish triumph: if I could overcome that adversity, why couldn't Dad?

That deepening winter, as always, the house grew bitterly cold. We had paraffin stoves in the hall and on the landing, and these filled the air with the spiritually consoling and slightly dizzying airport aromas of unburnt kerosene. But they added no general warmth whatever, and our bed linen felt like the winding sheets of the dead. In the morning, the inside of our east-facing windows were covered in a thick whorled layer of shimmering ice. I should emphasize that this wasn't hardship. It merely was, for we knew no other life. And thanks to Mum's untiring efforts, for the most part we were actually quite happy. Dad came home in time for Christmas, and he took me to Simpkin and James, Leicester's not ungallant attempt at a high-class food-and-drinks emporium. It smelt of ripe Stilton cheeses, old port, nuts and the sherry-soaked timbers of ancient casks. It was part of Dad's ritual every December to order the Christmas drinks there, including exotic liqueurs from Israel and Peru that would stay untouched in the sideboard for years.

On Christmas Eve it snowed, and Dad put on the gramophone Bing Crosby's 'Stille Nacht', and 'Adeste Fideles'. The carols rang through the house. I was perched on the windowsill on the landing just above a paraffin stove, gazing out onto Medina Road and watching the heavy snowflakes spiral suddenly into white existence in the glow of the street light at the corner of Buckminster Road. Despite the unending saga of Dad's illness, that evening I felt a special happiness. Dad was home, and surely now, all would soon be well, as winter passed and spring arrived.

A pleasing conjunction of my twin fantasies arrived that March, when a special Christ the King choir, of which I was (as usual) a much shamrock-bedecked member, joined in a St Patrick's Day concert in the De Montfort Hall. Also performing was a band from the United States Air Force base at Bruntingthorpe. We sang 'The Minstrel Boy', and everyone – the Americans included – joined in a magnificent 'Hail Glorious St Patrick'. My heart nearly exploded with joy.

By this time Mum had laid out my future with some care. As a lad of humble origin, Dad, I know, would have preferred a modest, local education. Mum felt otherwise. After Christ the King, I was to go to Wyggeston Grammar School, where I would stay for just two years, before moving to Ratcliffe, a Catholic public school in north Leicestershire. This would ensure both a Catholic education and an elevated social standing. My mother was a good woman, but something of a snob. I think she always hankered to reclaim some of the status that she had forfeited by marrying Dad.

Wyggeston was the greatest grammar school in all of Leicestershire: like public schools, it was divided into various 'houses', named after English martyrs of the reformed faith. My house, as I was to discover, was Latimer, after the Leicestershire-born cleric who was burnt for heresy by Queen Mary, right across from Balliol College Oxford, no doubt to remind up-and-coming students of the incendiary perils of religious dissent. Needless to say, since Wyggeston chose its pupils rather carefully, and moreover cherished its role in the Reformation, it did not regard itself as a mere prep school for a minor Catholic public school. My attendance at Wyggeston therefore required from me a pretence that I was going to remain a pupil there till I was eighteen.

By the humble standards of what I was used to, it was vast – a thousand pupils – and entirely male. For the first assembly, as for all those that followed, Catholics and Jews were told to wait outside. It wasn't discrimination. The school service was Protestant, from which we were excluded by the rules of our own religions. The very existence of 'Jews' came as a major surprise to me, for hitherto they had merely been an odd people in the Bible, along with Pharisees, Centurions and Samaritans – that any other of these almost mythical creatures should have turned up at Wyggeston would have seemed no more absurd. Equally surprising was their appearance: most looked markedly different from the Catholics, often with distinctive noses, and dark complexions, and, as I discovered, possessing strange names like Goldring and Goldstein. Yes, I know these are clichés: but clichés exist for a reason. So we non-Protestants stood together in the open yard, in orderly lines, being supervised by prefects of our own faiths. The school paths that morning were being relaid with tar, and the air was dense with the beguiling fragrance of hot naphthalene. An enormous pear tree dropped its fruit, one by one, in explosive splashes onto the ebony apron that had been laid the day before.

'Steady in the ranks,' a prefect commanded sardonically, meaning that the fruit was to remain where it lay. A huge fat pear plummeted through the foliage like an unlucky parachutist and landed several feet away from me. The prefect had turned his back and didn't see it. I stepped forward, retrieved it, and was back in position before he turned round. An invisible smile of triumph passed through the ranks of the boys, like a virus through a submarine. For a moment I was a minor hero. Afterwards, the boys came to inspect my pear. It was really vast and only slightly bruised, but it was delicious. Two smells are conjoined for ever in my memory banks, the champagne perry of bruised pear flesh and the heady naphtha of fresh tar.

In class I found myself sharing a double desk with a boy called Andrew Steele. That summer, Ann had been in Germany, and on her return had given me a biro marked 'Heidelberg', which I thought the very acme of sophistication. I now opened my new pencil case with all its exciting equipment: compass, protractors, set-square, pencils, fountain pen and my brilliant new Heidelberg biro. Steele – a thin, sandy-haired boy – reached over, grabbed my biro, stuck it up his nostril, and removed a huge gobbet of snot with it. He passed me back the biro, complete with bogey.

'There you are, you and your fúckin' 'Eidelberg biro.'

Well, really. I should have punched him there and then, but Christ the King had not bred aggression, and anyway, he wasn't small enough for me to employ such a dramatic foreign policy. So I wiped the precious biro on a piece of blotting paper, and set about ignoring him.

'Bet you don't know what fúck means.'

I continued to ignore him. At Christ the King I'd already heard the fantastic theory about the bits of the body that humans weed from being used for some incredible act that managed to be both disgusting and absurd.

'Fúck. It's wa' your dad and mam do w'en they gu t'bed.'

That Mum and Dad did such a thing was manifestly the most insane thing I had ever heard.

'That's rubbish,' I replied.

'No it in't,' said Steele. 'It's yooman nature. It's 'ow they mek babbies.' And he broke into song: 'Me Bonny lies over the ocean, Me Bonny lies over the sea. Me Daddy lies over me Mammy, And that's how they got little me.'

He clearly hadn't made this verse up. Could it be true? 'Do you know what cúnt means?' continued Steele.

'Of course I do. It's the crack where girls wee out of.'

'Not only that. It's where bebbies come out of.'

'Babies? How can they? There's no room!'

'Yes there is. There's a big 'ole.'

'Hole?'

'Ooh oh. An 'ole. A big un.'

And so that morning, through the first French and Latin and algebra classes of my life, I also had my first lessons in sex. It took me five years to reach the level of knowledge to allow me pass my O levels in the academic subjects, but by lunchtime I was nearly up to exam standard in most pelvic matters. They were only of clinical curiosity to me, though what homosexual men allegedly did to one another seemed perfectly impossible. But nonetheless, even that – *up their arses?* – was a kindred absurdity to the notion that my parents took pleasure from intermingling their urinary systems.

I soon learnt that being top of the class in almost everything at Christ the King counted for nothing at Wyggeston. All the boys there had passed the 11-plus exam, and as the main classical grammar school in Leicester, whose roots went back to Henry VIII's time, it had demanding traditions of scholarship. I was nowhere near top of the class, and in some areas was struggling, not least because I had grown inattentive. Wyggeston gave me vast amounts of homework, which I regarded as an outrageous violation of the entire purpose of home. So out of an indignant laziness, I rapidly lost contact with the smarter boys in the class. Had I feared Dad a little more, I might have been more a more diligent, but I had seen him weep too often to be scared of him. However, parsing and sentence analysis in English came naturally to me, and I was easily the best in the class, while in other areas I was merely middling – though it was studying Latin grammar that taught me the difference between 'I will' and 'I shall', a distinction that lit the sky like a comet.

Dad seldom angled any more, but he and I still went to Leicester City matches. I would now pay at the boys' turnstiles and join him in the grandstands where he had a season ticket, and where I squeezed in beside him. Such petty Irish lawlessness was so incomprehensible to the Leicester mind that quite simply, none of the ground stewards had a tactic to deal with it. Half-enviously, I would hear boys sitting on the pitch-side wall, chanting for Leicester City. Oh to be in a gang like that! Evenings drew in, and we would return home after the match in the half light, and soon in the dark. Together we would trudge towards the car on the rain-soaked pavement discussing the game as the grey vapours of a Midland twilight descended, and the smell of fish and chips and vinegar and coal smoke filled the air. He was always more scathing than I was of Leicester's performance, even in victory, whereas I took a boyish delight in merely being a supporter. I belonged, with the passion of the tribally committed. The blue of Leicester City was my colour, and the clodhopping bullocks with miners' boots on their feet and gums where their teeth should be, were my heroes.

Once, for an all-ticket cup match, when Dad's fluent frauds would have been unable to get me into the ground, he arranged for me to be brought into the stadium by a Scottish forward named Jimmy Walsh from Glasgow, whose family were his patients. I was so excited as I waited outside the players' entrance that I was sure I was going to wet myself. When he emerged, seeing a small boy there, he said, 'Agh anoo. I dinna ken yae nae hoo, oglouh ne'er aughtermuchtie stenhousemuir cowdenbeath wa hey?'

My knees nearly folded beneath me, my lungs went strangely airless. I was in the company of a soccer player who had once nearly played for the Scottish U21 B team! I was unable to speak.

'Cairngorm Ben Nevis och aye the noo, wee cooper o' Fife, hey nonnie nonnie no nay no, aye.'

I was still far too excited to reply. His brow furrowed. 'Are yee nae the doctor's bairn?'

The Rosetta Stone briefly flared within me. 'Sorry, sir. Yes, sir! Kevin, sir!'

'Gang agley whisht the noo, Kevin, Hogmanay, firth o' forth, jura, mugg, egg and rum, och aye the noo.'

Muttering amiably in the language that merely shares the name 'English' with the language I spoke but none of the contents, he led me through the bowels of the bus shelter that was the Leicester City Stadium.

'Clackmannan alloa mashie niblick forfar five fife four, way hey,' he continued conversationally, before taking me to Dad's seat in the stands. To be visibly escorted into the stadium by a Leicester City player, even if he was speaking Lappish, raised me to a lofty height well above the mere rabble surrounding me. I glowed with a plutonium pride that was not remotely diminished by the Carthaginian conquest of Leicester City that followed.

THE LITTLE ONES regularly answered the door to thoroughly embarrassed patients bearing urine samples in brown paper bags. I would always open the bag to check what it was, usually causing the donor to flee as if an air-raid siren had sounded. I decided one day to add spice to Dad's life by concocting a sample myself, made from one of the scores of empty bottles from Dad's pharmacy, and containing a mixture of water and a plausible quantity of orange squash. On the label, I scribbled something indecipherable to serve as the patient's name, and handed it over to Dad, reporting that a lady had asked me to give it to him.

He took it away for testing while I waited in the hall, then emerged, looking grave. He went to the only phone in the house, on the little table there, and began to dial a number.

'What is it Dad?'

He stopped dialling and looked at me. 'Mrs Simms' sample has lethal levels of sugar in it. She's dying. She could already be dead. I've got to ring the Royal Infirmary now. God almighty! How could I have missed all the symptoms?'

'What do you mean, Dad, Mrs Simms?'

'That's her sample. It has her name on it.'

A surge of panic took control of me. 'What do you mean, her name?'

He put the phone down and returned with the bottle, pointing at the label, and the hieroglyphic gibberish that I had scribbled, which by curious mischance actually looked like 'Mrs Simms'.

I managed to summon enough courage to confess all. Far being angry at me, Dad was delighted at my practical joke, but we solemnly agreed: no more japes involving patients' urine.

Our family life fell into predictable patterns. Sundays were always an early start at St Peter's, to which my mother now drove, if the verb 'drive' adequately conveys the series of intellectually disconnected vehicular episodes through which we passed between our home and our destination. She had been a left-handed child who had been made to write with her right hand, thereby irreversibly damaging her synchronizing skills. Car journeys with Mum at the wheel usually began and ended with prayers by her passengers, initially of petitions for divine mercy, and at the conclusion, a querulous, babbling gratitude at their safe deliverance. After Mass we would return for the great family meal of the week, Sunday morning breakfast, which was always the same: rashers of bacon, fried bread and eggs, toast and marmalade and tea. It lasted about an hour, before Dad would leave for eleven o'clock Mass, and the family would become molecular for the next two hours.

We called the midday meal 'dinner', and it was always a roast, with pudding to follow. This was an era of tinned foods for the masses, a legacy of the war, which I occasionally got at the Thoms' or Mark's: fruit salads that were a boiled soup of grapes and pears and tasted of cheap chewing gum, steak pies from Argentina containing fragments of carcass encased in floured lard, and corned beef that looked like the inside of a crashed bomber and tasted of earwax. But Mum allowed no such abominations on her table. She was true to her class. High tea took place in the evening, with scones, cakes and sponges. Then we would crowd round the biscuit tin of the television screen and watch until eight o'clock, when after evening prayers, the Little Ones would be sent to our beds, which usually felt as if they had just been used for storing the corpses from a North Sea trawler disaster.

I LIKED Wyggeston. I liked the boys: the aboriginal English stock, mostly sturdy, reliable and true. I liked the Jews too. They seemed different and almost exotic. They were industrious and discreet, aloof even, and they even kept their own company without being over-clannish. However, a couple of Jews were loud and extravagently self-confident, such as the endlessly charming Siegel, who, aged twelve, actually wore a tailored mohair overcoat over his school uniform, which he once tried to sell me.

At school meals I was on the 'float' because I didn't yet have a permanent table in the dining hall. The float waited outside until all the boys with allocated places were seated, and a senior boy commanding each table would stand if his table had a vacancy. The float would then charge in to find a place. As I rushed past a table, a fat and swarthy boy with sideburns cried 'Hoy', and gestured to an empty seat beside him. The senior boy was not standing. He looked at me and nodded. I took the empty space. After grace, which even we Catholics and Jews heard with bowed heads, I also offered thanks to my Samaritan. He was a chubby young bruiser called Pete Harvey a year older than me, who, being a Catholic, had seen the audacious deed with the pear on my first day and had marked me out. He effectively ran the table, the senior boy never standing whenever there was vacancy, so allowing Peter to choose his company from the float. Thus did I come to be the only first-year boy to be inducted into Pete Harvey's gang. Pete had Elvis Presley hair, winkle-picker shoes, deep brown eyes set in fat cheeks, and almost uniquely in those days, a belly. He could almost have been one of the extrovert Jewish, but since he was a Catholic I suspect his family were Italians or Spaniards who had anglicized their name. I had just been recruited into his gang – a real privilege. They always went to see Leicester City play at home, and he soon suggested I join them.

As we were getting ready the following Saturday morning to go the match, I told Dad I wouldn't be sitting with him in the stands, and would instead be joining my new friends on the terraces.

'But we always go together to the matches. It's our treat. Sure isn't that what football is all about, fathers and sons going to the matches together?'

All right, I agreed, but I did so with a telling gracelessness. Poor Dad knew that an epoch, already tiny in its duration, was now coming to an end. He told me soon that in future I should indeed join my friends, and he would see me afterwards. So I started to make my own way to Filbert Street, long before kick-off, with sandwiches and a flask, in order to join Peter Harvey's gang outside the ground, to play football, to drink pop, to eat fish and chips, and talk bawdy boy talk. Soon, I didn't even join him after the match, staying with the boys, while he went home alone. I was his friend, and like all his friends, I had abandoned him.

My knowledge of life was now growing exponentially, as too was the mythology of boyhood. I have no idea of what twelve-year-old Peter, the Artful Dodger, actually knew from his own personal experience, probably nothing, but he was the perfect oracle for transmitting the rumours about life that boys believed to be the truth. One sunny day after dinner, sitting in the long grass beside the playing fields, with grasshoppers chirruping around, Pete gave us all a seminar about sex, and male duty, which was to give a girl pleasure. The best way of doing that was to insert not one but two fingers.

'How you know when you're pleasing her?' I asked.

'They ge' rall wet and cúver yer finger in piss. And they always yell, "Oooo ya byoooty, MAAAM!" ' he declared solemnly.

'What?'

'Oo ah. When gels fetch off, they always say MAAAM! Same as when gels climb ropes. That's why súm gels' schools dún't have no ropes.'

'Wyggeston gels school 'ad to tek 'em down,' declared Phil Wilkinson knowingly.

'Cos gels were climbin' 'em th' 'ole time,' explained Pete, 'then fetchin' off and yellin', "Oooo ya byoooty, MAAAM", and then gerrin' stranded.'

'Ad to gerrin rúddy the fire brigade to gerrem down,' added Phil.

'Why do the girls scream for their mothers?'

Peter turned to his gang.

'E wants to know why gels fetching off screech for their mams.'

A roar of knowing laughter.

'There were a gels' borstal in Birmingham,' continued Pete, 'and the gels were inside for murder and rape and stúff and they 'adn't seen no blokes for years, and the local milk co-op 'ad a special lesbian milkman to deliver milk. But she got the flu, so some bloke were gev 'er milkround. And the poor fúcker cúm up the drive on 'is float, and the gels stopped 'is 'oss, and they pulled 'im dahn off the float, and they stripped 'im bare, and 'eld 'im dahn an' tyey took turns tossin' 'im off till 'e were passin' blood, and they kept tossin' 'im off till 'he bled to death.'

'Oo ya beauty,' said one of the boys in wonder. 'Worra way to go.'

'And that's 'ow dangerous gels can turn if they don't gerrit reg'lar,' admonished Peter, as grave as Aesop.

Wyggeston was a good school, with an Englishness I still admire. It had core values, all of them understated: of duty, of loyalty, of steadfastness and of modesty, as embodied in the school's most famous pupil, David Attenborough. Those qualities also informed how the boys played rugby. I was just about good enough to get into the First Year rugby team, primarily for my defensive skills. Tackling large boys, regardless of the weight or momentum, was something on which I prided myself. The Irish were always brave and true to their team, Dad had told me that, so I was going to be brave and true also. Stereotypes, even if false, can, by the mere alchemy of myth, make themselves come true. And else what is nationalism if not a mental carcinogen, capable of converting human tissue into a living replica of a fantasy?

My English teacher was an elderly man named Greenhaugh. One morning as he was writing on the blackboard, Andrew Steele knocked over a bottle of ink. The boy to my right spotted the accident and wordlessly passed me over a piece of blotting paper. I passed it equally silently to Steele, while listening to Greenhaugh talk with his back to us. Then, he put the piece of chalk on the rim beneath the blackboard, turned, and walked down the central aisle towards me. He paused before my desk and suddenly hit me very hard across the face with the full force of his open hand.

I blinked in astonishment and pain. I had never seen anyone hit like that, not even the worst boy in the class, and I was certainly not that. Greenhaugh brought his face close to mine, his pupils glinting with hatred, his breath stale. Then he hit me with his other hand, equally powerfully. He stepped back one pace, glaring at me. It was over. My face burned in agony, as if petrol had been ignited on it. Yet I felt relief. It was over. Monstrously unfair as it was, I had come through it.

I waited for him to turn and go back to his desk. Instead, he hit me again, but now even harder. A pause, before he slapped me with the other hand. Then the two hands, slowly, methodically, began smashing into my cheeks, one after the other, left, pause, right, left, pause, right, and all I could say to myself was: 'Do not cry. Be a man. Do not cry.'

One boy, Pete Winnick, had started counting, and was later to tell me that Greenhaugh hit me ten times on each cheek. And then, his shoulders hunched, he turned and slowly walked back to his desk, his gown billowing, while the class stayed as silent and unbreathing as medical students watching a heart transplant.

Do not cry, I intoned endlessly to myself. Do not cry.

And I didn't cry – well, not as such. A deep sob of shock came from my belly and my lungs, and filled the classroom's ghastly silence with the sound of innards heaving. I had no idea if Greenhaugh then proceeded with the remainder of his lesson. All I knew was that uncontrollable convulsions were erupting within my little body, making me first choke and then gag. In turn, like the blows that had preceded them: choke … gag … choke … gag. I knew, passionately, that a terrible injustice had been done, but why me? Even in childhood, amongst the shoals of disconnected facts and the fresh islands of knowledge that come floating into your ken, there's usually some sort of coherence to things, for even the most incomprehensible sea nonetheless observes certain oceanic laws. Events were seldom completely random and entirely without context, yet this criminal assault clearly was.

The bell rang for lunchtime, but no one moved. The boys sat on, silently listening to my deep, uncontrollable, convulsive sobs.

'Go!' said Greenhaugh finally. 'Get out! The lot of you! Unless you all want detentions, get out now – except you, Myers. You stay where you are!'

The boys didn't move. I looked up at Greenhaugh as he glared around him. His face was grey. His pupils shone like black stars through his spectacles.

'It's all right. Myers here has learnt his lesson. I shan't be repeating it. It's not necessary, Myers, is it?'

I choked. 'No sir.'

Wordlessly, the boys left. Greenhaugh came down to me.

'You got what you deserved.'

I managed to control my sobbing to speak. 'But I was only passing Sharpe some blotting paper because he'd spilt some ink.'

'Ha! A likely story.'

He gestured at his spectacles on his face. 'You thought I couldn't see you because my back was turned. But I could – in the reflection in my lenses! I see everything! The whole time! You won't ever get the better of me, boy.'

'I wasn't trying to, sir.'

'I tell you what I'll do. I won't make a complaint about your intolerable behaviour to the head. Other teachers have been complaining, you know. That could mean expulsion. So we'll let by bygones be bygones. There now! What do you say to that?'

'Yes sir. Thank you sir.'

And thus enlisting the grateful victim in a conspiracy to protect the culprit, he left the classroom; and there I stayed, weeping throughout lunchtime. That evening, I lied to Dad about the angry blotches on my cheeks. I said they came from rugby. Overnight, my face then turned swollen and blue. My class teacher, Mr Day, asked if I was all right. I said yes. Small lies usually suffice if no one thinks to enquire forcefully. The one thing I should have done was the one thing that I didn't do, which was to have told Dad. But it was not just his illness that prevented me from doing so. Such was the discrete, autonomous culture of boys that I dreaded my parents getting involved in any school matters. Let it pass, I told my young self, and pass it did. No. No it didn't.

To my joy, I discovered that Peter Harvey's set of twelve-year olds were the ones making all the noise during Leicester City's matches. Inadvertently, I had joined the best gang in the stadium. For the first time in my life, I had status. Pete's gang would quite casually go by train to Birmingham, Nottingham, Wolverhampton to support Leicester City, and I began to go with them. They behaved like small adults, playing cards for money, and some smoked, though only when the railway guard wasn't around. A couple of the boys didn't like me because they thought I was too lah-di-dah, but when one said as much, Peter Harvey cuffed him.

'Shút the fúck úp, you. Kev's me mate, Kev is. You don't wan' 'im around, then fúck off wi' yer. Scarper.'

We regarded ourselves as Leicester City's main fans, for we spent more time outside the ground before a match than we did inside. In recent years, Leicester City supporters have – with good reason – become passionately vocal for a team that has been extraordinarily successful. But in those more inhibited days, Leicester folk were usually as demonstrative as mourners at the funeral of an Amish elder, watching the game with near silent stoicism. Pete could lead us in what we were sure was the coolest, most riveting and blood-curdling team chant of all time.

'We yell, we yell, and when we yell, we yell like hell, and this is what we yell. L-E-I-C-E-S-T-E-R, LEICESTER!' finishing with a triumphant roar, as if the Amish widow had just taken her knickers off. We were sure that we were the life and soul of Filbert Street, as indeed, we probably were.

Not content with the kick-arounds outside Filbert Street and Wyggeston being rugby only (a sport he detested), Pete formed his own soccer club, Humberstone Athletic. It was while I was playing for it that I saw the very first professional sporting 'dives', by Pete himself of course, which he performed whenever anyone successfully tackled him. He would instantly throw his hands up into the air, as if he had just been shot through the ribcage, and collapsing, would roll around in agony, until either he got the free kick, or grew bored. Moments later, he would be once again waddling around the pitch, like a penguin chasing mice. This, now, was long before adult footballers had begun to 'dive'. With the modest exception of some obstetric events on Palm Sunday 1947, I was never present for the birth of anything of importance in this world, save the professional foul, or 'a Pete Harvey', as we called it.

In my second year, when Pete Harvey had moved out of Lower School and Wyggeston's rules meant that I was not allowed to talk to him, I got to know and like boys in my own year: Des Berry, who became my best friend, Colin Hayes, Doug Probin, Vivian Sherlock and others. They were admirable young lads, whom I liked and respected enormously. There was an exception, however – for despite its rigorous selection process, Wyggeston had just accepted, as a late-entry pupil, the star delinquent of both Hazeldean High School and Christ the King

The most awesome boy in school was a Jewish thug in the fifth form named Spielberg. He was most un-Jewish. Jews never hit anyone, but he seemd to hit people ever day. Naturally, he was the leader of a gang of a gang, but mostly of non-Jews (a gang composed entirely of Leicester Jews would have been intimidating as a sewing circle of very elderly nuns). His dominance of the Fifth Form was a fact of life that never troubled us until he led his gang out of the Middle School playground and began to tour the junior playgrounds, clearly looking for prey. Television programmes by Wyggeston's most famous ex-pupil David Attenborough have since shown us how chimpanzees go on the warpath – the strange shambling lope, the odd set to the shoulders, the beetling brows, the jaws half open. This was just how Spielberg's admirably ecumenical Judaeo-Christian gang behaved, and they would, frankly, have been quite terrifying if they were after just any First Year rhesus monkey such as myself. They stalked right by me, their eyes peering left and right. Yes, they were looking for none other than Edward Warwick, who with an untypical prudence, parked himself outside the office of the headmaster of the junior school, Nobby Clark.

The next day Edward Warwick appeared in public with two Jewish prefects beside him as his bodyguards, presumably because of some cultural power they might have had over Spielberg. One of them was Simmonds, who had minded us Catholics and Jews on our first morning. This protection, alas, was not accepted with the grace and diplomacy that it surely merited. At the midday break, Edward Warwick walked up to the boundary with the middle school playground, making monkey gestures, and shouting:

'Eh up, Spielberg, you stoopid fúcking twat, who's the big boy now, you great fat Jewish wanker.'

Not even a veteran observer of Warwick's capers could be optimistic about the outcome, because Spielberg was not merely violent, but cunning too. Sure enough, Spielberg's gang soon ambushed Warwick on his way home, his bodyguards off duty, and so comprehensively that he ended up in hospital. He left Wyggeston, and also, my schooldays for ever. Meanwhile, Spielberg was allowed to remain at Wyggeston solely to do his exams. He was, it was generally agreed, both lazy and stupid, and was widely expected to fail his all O levels, after which a spectacular career in crime naturally awaited him. Instead, he got nine grade As. I have no idea what became of him: head of Mossad, probably.

The Wyggeston swimming pool was only in use in the summer, when it was freely available at the end of any day, and one unusually hot evening Des Berry and I went for a long and delicious dip. The tuck shop was still open and so when we'd finished, and we went and bought a lime ice lolly each. As we walked up the tree-lined driveway to the bus stop, Des turned to me said, 'It's true what they say, you know. Your schooldays are the happiest time of your life.'

We put our arms over one another's shoulders, the way boys used to, and headed off homeward. But I could not share his unalloyed happiness. I knew that my time at Wyggeston was coming to an end, but I didn't dare tell anyone, least of all Des Berry. I was really happy there and I was deeply ashamed to be leaving both the school and the many boys that I liked. Moreover, I knew all the implications of boarding school in their minds, that I would become hoity-toity and aloof. I know that Dad really didn't want me to leave Wyggeston, but a family tradition had been set by my brothers Bill and David.

One day, Des Berry came up to me and said very coldly, 'Is it true you're leaving?' I couldn't speak, I was so ashamed. I just nodded. 'And you didn't even have the bloody decency to tell me. Who'd you tell? Pete Harvey?'

'No one ...'

'Huh! Ain't we good enough for you no more?'

Actually, they were far, far better for me than what lay ahead.

Nine

RATCLIFFE COLLEGE was founded by Italian missionaries of the Rosminian Order in the mid nineteenth century. They had initially started proselytizing in the villages of north Leicestershire, under the aegis of the de Lisle family, recusant Catholic gentry whose estates and titles had miraculously survived the Penal Days. In time, the Rosminians started two schools in north Leicestershire: a preparatory school, Grace Dieu (pronounced Grey Stew) for boys from eight to twelve, and Ratcliffe, for boys from thirteen to eighteen.

Ratcliffe's school buildings and church were Victorian High Gothic, and had been designed by the great architect Pugin. They contained long stone-columned marble-floored corridors gracefully placed around a classic quadrangle. I had noticed whenever visiting David and Bill that Ratcliffe clearly had a pleasing atmosphere. The boys seemed noisily happy, and the school even smelled nice, of beeswax and contentment. Though I regretted leaving Wyggeston, I had no particular dread of Ratcliffe. However, as Mum and Dad drove me there, I felt ill with apprehension. I was leaving them for the first time; an eviscerating prospect. Our final moments together were spent in the Victorian mock-baronial front hall, as Dad played with his car keys, and Mum stifled her tears. I was introduced to the head teacher of the junior school, Brother Duffy, a cheerful young man, and he shook my hand solemnly before moving off to meet other parents and their sons. I was wearing a grey flannel suit, and with my first long trousers, which I hated. I cherished the feckless freedom of boyhood, of which short trousers were the offical uniform.

A bell rang across the school. Brother Duffy waited a moment and then clapped his hands. 'Apologies, ladies and gentlemen, but it's time for parents to go. Make your farewells brief, if you please.' Jointly snuffling mothers and boys kissed one another farewell, while pale fathers looked on. Then the parents shuffled outside. More farewells in the warm early autumn sunlight, before the mothers performed the final hugs and kisses. Dad looked at me, and I could sense his longing for us to embrace. But I was performing my little juvenile imitation of manliness, so we stayed apart. Few things sting in later years than the love unshown when it was so yearned for. So, we pupils stood in front of the cut-stone front doorway, inhaling the fragrance of the immaculate rose gardens, as we watched our parents make their way to the jumble of badly parked cars. Motherly hands waved from open windows, and then, car by car, and pair by pair, parents vanished down the tree-lined driveway, leaving us alone with one another and our teenage years. Departure is a key ingredient of all life, and adulthood is shaped from a multitude of farewells. Yet even with this wisdom, the acute sadness of that moment strikes me still, as I think of the extraordinary sense of loneliness that filled my young soul. And as my parents drove away from me, the trembling meniscus on my pupils finally broke.

Of course, such farewells are preludes to discovery, meeting new people, eating strange new boarding-school food, sharing a washroom with forty other boys, sleeping in a bed in a dormitory, which was governed over by a prefect called Day, who had his own room. In the morning, I went to Mass and took communion in the dark and Gothic Victorian church. It was dark and brooding and beautiful, lined with wood panels, and above them the walls were either papered or painted in sumptuously dark maroon, deep cobalt and rich old gold. And of course an old friend awaited me here also: a trip to the communion rail added another mortal sin to add to the hundreds I had already racked up, another reassurance that my immortal soul was doomed.

After breakfast, which consisted of grease sculpted into food shapes, the entire school gathered for the first time at assembly, conducted by Claud Leetham, the headmaster. Claud – as he was universally known – had a great mane of white hair and a huge crimson nose, the deep rubicundity of which was enriched by his habit of endlessly stroking it. He spoke with a deeply plummy accent, accompanied by random interjections. His opening words went something like: 'I want to say hello to all you chaps woof who survived the summer break, woof! And of course, to welcome all the new boys. I should make it plain to youngsters, this is a simple school with simple ways, woof! Our job is not so easy – it is to turn you young savages into ah Catholic gentlemen, and yours is not much easier. It is to pretend to be ah young gentlemen, woof! As for you newcomers who want to be ah gentlemen: take a look at the ah fifth form, and do the ah opposite, woof!'

Laughter and good-natured cheers followed, and Claud beamed beatifically down on us, running one hand through his mane of hair and rubbing his enormous beacon-like nose with the other. 'Ratcliffe isn't ah nationally famous, but you can be sure it is famous in God's eyes, and ah especially in the eyes of His Blessed Mother, woof! Our intention is to produce ah Catholic English gentlemen, and to those of you who are Welsh or Scottish or Irish, my condolences, woof!'

Again he beamed, and everyone laughed. 'We have some ah French boys here too. Vooz ett ah beeyen vennoo, maysewers. May ah suvenong Agincourt, woof!'

More laughter followed this excruciating French and the injunction to remember Henry V's victory, especially since it was quite clear that Claud was speaking with his tongue firmly in his cheek. Then the older boys led us in the hymn that was used for all assemblies: '*Salve Regina, Mater Misericordiae, Vita Dulcedo, Et spes nostra …*'

And so the term unfolded before our compliant and unchallenging eyes, as the sponge of our brains absorbed all that was laid before it, the academic stuff as much as the rites and rules of Ratcliffe. Two taboos were instantly imprinted on my mind: 'snitches', boys who informed on fellow pupils, were scum. Barely less scummy than them were 'licks', boys who ingratiated themselves with teachers. We also had to learn two songs, '*Salve Regina*', and the school anthem, '*Floreat Ratcliffia*'. The former we heard daily, and the latter, a very ancient anthem of very recent composition, was sung seriously just once a year, during the school banquet on the Feast of the Immaculate Conception on 8 December.

One morning Claud Leetham spoke to us with a graver-than-usual manner: 'Some of you might be ah aware of a certain trial in London, woof,' he boomed lugubriously. He was wrong there. Every single boy had been avidly following the newspaper reports of the *Lady Chatterley* trial, and the delicious, if asterisked, words that had actually been pronounced in the court. 'I regret to inform you ah that the book has not been banned by law, woof. But let me ah assure you that I am ah banning it here in this school. Any boy caught reading it shall be instantly expelled, unless ah specifically authorized by me in advance for solely scholarly reasons. And this other fellow, the new chap, James Bond: he's doubly banned and no exceptions. Woof!'

Lady Chatterley never entered the bootleg circuit of banned books in Ratcliffe, but the Bond books did. The sexual scenes are almost invisible to today's reader, but back then they were incredible. 'Her nipples were hard with desire …' resonated like a bomb in the whispered exchanges in the common room. What could that actually mean? Women didn't feel desire, did they? I had never really analysed the implications of Pete Harvey's bawdy stories, other than they seemed rude and funny. Was this how life actually was?

However, the coming world of adulthood was glimpsed only occasionally through the woodland trees of daily life. I was better at class than I had been at Wyggeston, but academic standards were lower. I could still hold my own on the rugby pitch, even though I remained small just as adolescence was arriving for many other boys like a deforming plague. We played on a remote pitch, far from the school, called 'the airfield'. It had been an RAF training base during the war, and it was said an Old Ratcliffian bomber pilot had circled the school one night, flashing his name, his school number and SOS signal, looking for permission to land. None came, and in time his plane vanished. But it later transpired he had in fact been shot down over Germany, and only his ghost had returned. The tale was certainly a fabrication, but it still flourished because it was the kind of myth that boys love.

One day in November I read in *The Daily Telegraph* that an Irish army patrol had been massacred in the Congo. To my mind, Ireland was still a paradise beyond the sea, where no harm befell anyone; and Irish soldiers, as my father had told me, were the best there were. That such men, yes, Irishmen, could be slaughtered in such a systematic butchery seemed utterly incredible, a violation of all that was right. It was just after lunch. I sat in the corner of the common room, in tears, as if family members had been slain. The bells rang for classes. I couldn't take the newspaper with me, so I put it on the top of an old locked wardrobe in the common room, which that term had never been opened.

That evening I went to retrieve the *Telegraph*, and standing on a chair, felt along the top of the wardrobe. I found the newspaper, but I also found a key. It was so obvious, of course, to have hidden a key there, but sometimes even the obvious escapes detection. I opened the wardrobe, and there in a stack was a collection of magazines from the First World War. The bedtime bell was just going, and I grabbed a handful, and later in bed opened one. I found myself looking at a page of photographs of some recent victims of battle. Not long before their deaths they had gazed directly into the camera. Now they gazed directly at me. Those faces, those eyes – they were just like the face and the eyes of Day, the prefect who was that very second sauntering up and down the dormitory with a casual and effortless authority.

That was it. That was war. Not grown men, or fully mature adults, but instead, teenagers like Day here, fresh-faced, handsome, genial and decent. One face – wide-eyed, trusting, doomed – struck me in particular. It was of Albert Ball VC, who was educated at Bloxham School, against which I had just played rugby. I kept turning the pages, and was next arrested by a photograph of a scholarly looking man wearing rimless spectacles, and with a name that seemed familiar. I pored long over it, before remembering. It was of Father Willie Doyle SJ, a chaplain killed in action, August 1917, whom my father had mentioned all those years before. The caption said he had been recommended for a Victoria Cross. I scanned the details of Father Doyle's life, just beneath the picture. He had been educated at Clongowes Wood College, in Ireland, and also at Ratcliffe College, Leicestershire. A lightning bolt struck me in my bed.

This Willie Doyle might have slept in this dormitory, or studied in my classroom, or played cricket and rugby on the green pitches surrounding the school. It was another epiphany, and its impact on me has lasted to this day. Indeed, without too much of an exaggeration, it could be said, in time, to have had an impact on the way that Ireland finally came to remember the Irish dead of the twentieth century. Certainly, the icy electricity that tingled through my body that evening was to change my view of history, of war, and over the years, of myself.

One day I was called into Father Hastings' room and given an utterly incomprehensible talk about birds and their nests. After a while, I said, 'Excuse me, father, are you trying to tell me about sexual intercourse?'

'Ah, good, that's that then. You may go now.'

One adolescent initiation rite had thus been passed. Another was to come: the cane, known at Ratcliffe as the 'swish', for which a sentencing teacher would write a 'note' to the head of the junior school.

We all knew the punishment tariff for various offences, and reading in class was guaranteed to win you a 'note', which was communication at its most economical: a piece of paper to be taken to the head of the lower school simply with a number on it: 4 or 6. Our Latin master was an elderly, short-sighted former Church of England clergyman named Hacker, with a big nose, huge spectacles and extraordinarily bad breath. He would sometimes sit beside me on my bench to examine my work, his arm round me, breathing heavily. Occasionally, he would rest his chin on my shoulder and sigh. The sexuality of all this was neither explicit nor in doubt.

He was less cuddly when he found me reading a Hammond Innes novel during class, and he gave me a note. I opened it as I walked the short distance to Duffy's office. It could be worse: 4. I knocked on the door.

'Enter.'

I walked in and silently passed Duffy the note. He opened it.

'What were you doing?'

'Reading in class, sir.'

He nodded and went over to and opened the punishment cupboard. There was a line of canes within in a frame, like snooker cues, each presumably graded according to the gravity of the crime. All of them were far thicker than the garden cane that I had expected to see. He took one from the centre, which suggested mine was a middle-ranking offence. It was alarmingly thick, with an ornate brass ferrule. Yes, someone actually *manufactured* this device, but had gone to some trouble to make it look attractive. This was a glimpse of an adult world even more mystifying than nipples hard with desire. He smote the air with two practice strokes: *swish swish*. He then made me kneel on all fours. 'Ready Myers?'

'Sir.'

The next moment the cane hit my bottom. The pain was astounding: it was in a different realm from anything else that I had ever felt. It was if a red hot flail had burnt deep into my buttocks and my brain: twin lances of unspeakable agony at either end of my torso. The effect was shockingly complete: I was cured of all reading-in-class habits for ever. But of course, that was irrelevant. Three more strokes still to come. I prayed to God that I would have the strength not to cry or sob and give any sign of weakness, and I waited and waited for the next blow.

When it did, it was, incredibly, far worse than the first. My buttock and my brain were boiling cauldrons of a deeply complex agony that had been caused by a simple length of bamboo (though with an attractive ferrule at the top). My skin felt as if I had sat on a gas cooker. My muscles were as bruised as if they had been hit with a spade. Even my bones deep in my buttock had, outraged, registered the blows. My brain was faithfully echoing each explosion of pain within its own cerebral valley.

The third was worse, beyond all words. The fourth completed my journey into a realm of agony far vaster than my little body or hapless mind could comprehend. There was no scale here, no proportion, but a galactic pain within the small thimble that was me.

I rose slowly, fresh agonies erupting the length of my body from my scalded buttocks. I said nothing, praying with a passion that I had never known before not to cry.

'Well done Myers,' said Duffy, shaking my hand. 'You may go now.' I hobbled out to the deserted boys' toilets, took down my trousers and pants and, craning my neck, could see my buttocks in the mirror. There were four raging rainbows across my bottom, the one colour missing being green, though it would no doubt follow. Blood was bubbling through the bruises and dribbling down my legs My underpants were already sodden and bright red. I mopped at my wounds with the shiny, useless toilet paper that had the absorbency of silver foil, and each attempt to staunch the flow of blood merely added to the pain. Finally, I padded the inside of my underpants pants with folded-over sheaths of paper and then returned to class. I emitted a crunching sound as I sat down.

When class was finished, Hacker came and sat beside me, and put his arm around me.

'I am sorry, dear boy, so desperately, desperately sorry.'

Tears were in his eyes and his breath smelt like a morgue on a hot day in Madagascar.

'It's all right, sir.'

He cuddled me closer, panting, bathing me in his fragrance of rotting cadavers. A tear trickled down his cheek. He moved his lips closer to me. For one hideous moment, I thought he was going to kiss me. Instead, he rose, and sobbed; 'You are a fine, decent lad. And so brave, so brave.'

As much in fear of his simpering, libidinous contrition as of the swish itself, I never read again in class – however, if anyone could have driven me to it, it was Frettie Fox, the maths teacher. Frettie was Irish, and easily the most boring man in the school. He could work his way into your brain like a weevil, where he would fuck with your inner clock. Each of his classes was a droning torment without apparent cease.

On Sundays, several priests would concelebrate High Mass, and we would never know which of them was going to give the sermon. The best start to the Mass was a Foxless one, but an air of foreboding always filled the church if Frettie Fox emerged from the vestry in the procession to the altar. If he got up to read the epistle or the gospel, there would be an audible sight of relief, because this meant that he would not say the sermon. But if he moved towards the pulpit after the gospel, the entire church, including the statue of the Virgin Mary, would audibly groan, for we knew we were in for forty-five minutes of a Frettie sermon. This was not forty-five minutes in human time, but as measured in Pluto, where a year is 245 of our years, and a minute endures a comparable elongation. Frettie always spoke without notes, unleashing his evil weevils into some 400 brains, without mercy, pause or compassion. I do not know why we didn't all become Muslims, or why Class 5C (the thickest and most irredeemable savages in the school) didn't beat him to death and barbecue his bones. Yet somehow or another Frettie was spared this fate, and he continued to inflict his Plutonic sermons on us throughout my school days, after which he ran off with a woman, God bless her, and – quite incredibly – sired many children by her.

I was familiar with our history teacher, Bert Orton, from his visits to our home, triggered initially by the brilliance of Bill, my oldest brother. My parents and he had become friends of a sort. I knew he was eccentric, but until my first class, I had no idea how much. After we had all given him our names, he began to prowl around the class like a cat, miaowing. Then he squatted down on the floor, and with a single leap, bounded vertically onto his desk, on which he hopped backwards and forwards, stroking his face with feline delicacy. Then he leapt down again. A moment later, he began to teach us history, scribbling dates on the blackboard, and finishing off his handiwork with a little sketch of a kitten in the bottom right-hand corner. He addressed each boy he spoke to as 'pussy cat', but not in any compromising or improper way. He was both very mad and very good.

One third of the way through the first term, I was allowed out for a day for the first time. One Sunday morning, I walked out of the front door of the school, and there, standing in the bleak north wind that in November blows over the high wolds of Leicestershire, was Mum. My heart thudded with joy, and for once as she drove me home I barely worried about her driving. I had never felt such love for Medina Road as I did when I entered the kitchen, where the beef was already roasting, and the house seemed so warm and welcoming. Dad was in the sitting room, smoking, and overjoyed to see him, I walked up and kissed him. I never wanted to leave home or him ever again, but that evening I did.

The entire Catholic population of the world was transfixed that autumn by the ermergence of John K. Kennedy as a potential US president. Catholicism was for me a two-fold identity: it was an expression of both my religion and my Irishness, and John F. Kennedy was therefore no more or less than a moneyed extension of the Myers family. His tribe was ours; it was simple. However, even the most Anglo-Saxon of Catholics at Ratcliffe supported Kennedy. Ours was an intensely tribal world, and the greatest tribe in the world was defined by our adherence to Rome.

Fridays were set aside for confession, and for me, a weekly descent farther into the pit of hell. On Saturday morning we had classes, and in the afternoon, rugby, followed by cold showers then tea, after which we would huddle round the radiators as night fell, and chat chastely: there were no Peter Harveys at Ratcliffe. Then the bell would ring for rosary, with services for the upper and lower schools. Soon the strange vocal rhythms of two columns of boys walking and praying in parallel corridors would fill the Gothic roof spaces like rival incantations across an alpine valley. The Saturday supper was prepared in advance so as to allow the mostly Sicilian staff an evening off, and was, incredibly, even worse than the meals through week: usually a slice of cold ham and sodden, refried chips that oozed grease as if squeezed from a putrifying corpse. Unspeakable and usually uneatable, though of course, we ate it. After this sumptuous banquet would come the weekly film in the gym, of irreproachable chastity, naturally, and watched by the entire school and community.

On Sunday we had an extra half an hour's sleep, and then rose and donned a black jacket and a white shirt with detachable studs – a humble imitation of the Eton collar. Breakfast, consisting of fat in its many forms, was followed by High Mass at ten. This lasted around two hours, and provided it was Foxless, it was often quite wonderful: the immaculately attired concelebrants would move in synchrony around the sanctuary while the main priest delivered the plainchant words, the Rosminian choir sang the chorus, and the boys' choir would usually offer a Bach or Mozart or Beethoven or Britten Mass. I shall forever be indebted for the music that was unveiled before my ears each Sunday in Pugin's magnificent pseudo-Gothic Victorian pile, while the incense rose into the dark vault of the roof and the sweetest human sound known to human ears, boys' voices, rang from the choir loft behind us.

Sunday lunch was a deformed and grotesque parody of the family equivalent, all tallow, starch, suet and gruel, as if barrack life from the Second World War was now our permanent condition. Yet despite this proteinless, vitamin-free diet the hormone train of adolescence daily unloaded its cargo of broken voices and ungainly, unmannered growth on my fellow pupils. Hitherto elegant companions of the changing-room, once so pink and chaste and epicene, would almost overnight be transformed into oafish, libidinous trolls, as septic spots and bristles erupted on cheek and chin, thigh bones lengthened regally and the soft green penile cress of boyhood turned into a burly lolling manliness, cushioned on a mattress of public hair. Behaviour changed too: mumbling incoherence and wild, unseemly cackles displaced the pleasant fluency and easy wit of late childhood. But not for me. My body was still a model of elfin smoothness, my male parts like bald pink fledglings slumbering in their little nest.

Dad had a huge female cousin who once visited us from Iowa: she had grown six inches after she'd got married, and I became fixated with that possibility happening to me any day now. No doubt I would have been bullied had I not already developed a considerable reputation for – oh dear me, how do I write this? – physical courage. I had taken up boxing, in part because of Dad's professed admiration for boxers. And I agreed, it was manly to take the blows and not complain. My delusions about 'Irishness' were confirmed by the presence in every single weight category of one of the Gallagher brothers, sons of a Birmingham builder and his heroic wife. With a commendable concern for the future of Ratcliffe boxing, the gallant Mrs Gallagher expressed a little one approximately every eleven months or so, guaranteeing that each school year, from the Lower Third to the Upper Sixth, had its very own boxing Gallagher, identikit Mayo bruisers with cheery grins, broken noses, and haymaker right hands. Not just the Irish adorned the boxing club; so did a lanky Nigerian named Emmanuel Adesina, whose arms were so long that his opponents were usually felled by a right hand that uncoiled with a lazy, deadly ease just as they were doing their inaugural mid-ring skip. He was known throughout the school as 'Sambo'. Even then, that word was generally unacceptable, so I asked him if he objected to the name. 'Why should I? No one means to insult me. It's just a word. Anyway, I'm the only boy in the school, beyond all question, that everyone else knows.'

I also had a reputation on the rugby pitch for tackling all comers, no matter their weight, and even when they charged head on and at full speed towards me. I might be carried back ten feet by the momentum, but I would usually bring the opponent down. In that first term, I was twice knocked out cold in tackles, and on both occasions resumed playing the moment when I gained consciousness. The much-dreaded match against Wyggeston finally came. My former schoolmates were not hostile, but nor were they friendly. I don't think they could really work out what was going on. In their eyes Ratcliffe was a third-rate school, so what was I, of all people, doing there? Had I not been one of them? Ratcliffe was routed, of course, and making a desperate tackle upon some departing heels of another try scorer, I was caught in the eye by a boot. Dad was watching keenly from the touchline, so I played on. His good opinion and the honour of Ireland were at stake. That evening my eye erupted, as if a purple cricket ball had taken its place. Prefects and teachers came to my dormitory to admire it. Nowadays I would probably be kept in hospital overnight and barred from playing for a month. But I was pleased and proud. Dad could only have been impressed by my courage.

I know now what my larger problem was. I believed. I accepted the rules of my school, as I did of my Church and of my family. I was credulous and naive and all in all, really quite decent. But then decency was a norm – most of the boys at Ratcliffe tried to live by the school rules, even when their bodies were engulfed and engorged by rampaging testosterone. There was a fundamental goodness about my teenage peers, which came down to the three Ds: duty, decency, daring. These were fine English concepts to raise boys to, a public-school refinement of the warrior-band ethos of the palaeolithic. They went into the making of me, and in due course, the unmaking.

Ten

BY THE TIME I entered my second term I had become extremely religious, and with that deepening sense of piety and devotion had come an even greater sense of the eternal horrors that my immortal soul should certainly endure were I to die unshriven. It is nowadays simply impossible to convey what this actually meant to me psychologically, with the absolute certainty that I would suffer unspeakable physical and mental torment, without respite, for all eternity. That such a belief might be demented rubbish is neither here nor there. It was what my young mind believed, and the burden on that mind grew heavier the more deeply religious I became.

The annual 'retreat' was the high point in Ratcliffe's religious year. A retreat was a period spent in prayer and contemplation and religious celebration, without social conversation or full meals. At the frugal collations in that Easter Week, excerpts were read aloud from the biography of the English martyr, Blessed Edmund Campion, and his trials and tribulations as he evaded the anti-Catholic forces of the English queen, but never, of course, losing his loyalty to England or his monarch. Prayers echoed along the cloisters throughout the day. We ate bread for lunch and listened to tales of the religious patriotism of Campion and his fellow martyrs, and the delirium caused by perpetual hunger was reinforced by a constant repetition of plainsong and chanted invocation. By the end of the first day I was in a state of spiritual ecstasy. Maundy Thursday was my fourteenth birthday, and I rose that morning, sure that I was close to resolving the torment that had been burning within me for so long. After morning Mass, and a breakfast of dry bread and tea, pupils were allowed to attend a plainsong service in the church or partake of religious reading. I went to the church, where the Rosminian choir was singing the Maundy antiphons, and gradually realized that as I was now fourteen years old, it was finally my duty to break free from the terrible sin that might soon cast my soul into perpetual damnation.

In the main corridor leading to the lower school, Father Nann, head of the upper school, was leading a group of boys in the rosary. When he had finished and had kissed his beads, I said I'd like to have a word with him. He turned, and gestured for me to follow, so that in a crowded corridor, we were alone. I asked him if would hear my confession.

'Of course,' he said. 'You're Myers, aren't you?'

'Yes, Father. Can you hear it now, please?'

'I'm hearing confessions at two. I'm sure it will wait.'

A frugal lunch then followed for those who were capable of eating. I was not. Doom of kind, I was sure, awaited me. I feared I might even face expulsion for having lied in confession, but I knew that I had to do this. Lunch over, I hastened to the church, and was appalled to discover the senior school had finished eating before us, and ten boys were kneeling in the queue for Father Nann. The line between us seemed to diminish with archaeological slowness. A question tolled within me, like bell sounding my doom: what if Nann decided that my sin was too huge for him to absolve? What if I were ejected from the confessional in disgrace? Finally my turn came, my bowels like water as I entered the wooden box wherein Nann waited.

All film and television enactments of confession portray the priest calling the penitent 'my child'. That is a complete fiction. 'Child' is a term of affection. It does not convey the awful imbalance of power that any despot would envy. On the one hand, in that small coffin there is – apparently – the total God-given authority of the priest to deny absolution to the imperfect penitent or to make the most appalling judgment upon his sins. Opposite kneels this broken creature whose presence in that timber tomb is proof of his or her total submission to the priestly authority.

Nann listened in silence while I told him of my wicked ways: how I dipped my finger in the sugar bowl before taking Holy Communion but had not then confessed my evil, evil crime, not just once but repeatedly; and then, worst of all, I had received the once-in-a-lifetime sacrament of confirmation while my soul was steeped in a sewer of mortal sin.

'I see,' he said, then allowing a silence settle. My body ceased to metabolize, as even the valves in my heart paused to hear what was coming next.

'Your scruples,' he said finally, 'do you credit, but you have been worrying unnecessarily. Mother Church is not the stern creature you imagine her to be. And God always understood your innocence. Don't be afraid of dealing with the truth. It can never harm you. You are a good boy, and you are to worry no more. I want you to say just one Hail Mary in penance for your sins, and I want you to remember me particularly in your prayers, if you would be so good.'

And that is indeed what priests would sometimes do: as a statement of abject humility, and a rejection of the absolutism that lay at their command, they would ask you to pray for them, to remind you that they were sinners too, equal to us poor penitents in the eyes of God.

I did not leave that confessional: I departed on wings of gossamer grace, my heart singing with silent joy. That day, I had just received the best birthday present ever. I stayed in a condition of unparalleled ecstasy that evening as the shades of nights descended in Pugin's old church and we commemorated the Last Supper, the tears of Gethsemane, the cock crowing thrice, and the betrayal and arrest of Jesus, the Saviour of All Mankind.

The next morning was Good Friday, the darkest day in the Christian calendar, and, as we were taught, the darkest day in the history of the world, the day when our beloved Redeemer was tortured and murdered, so that He might save my soul. And no, I do not understand any of it now, but I understood it fully then. I was brimming with emotions of joy and of religious passion as the Rosminian voices, those strong baritones and sweet tenors, led the school through the haunting plainchant rhythms: '*Dies Irae / Dies Illa / Solvet saeclum in favilla / Tested David cum Sybilla*' ('Day of wrath, oh wrathful day, turn to merest ashes, the direst words of David the psalmist and Sybil the soothsayer'). They were no fools, those founding fathers of church music. They knew where the soul lived, and how susceptible it was to the seductions of plainchant and the siege gun of sonorous repetition. And then later came the bizarre hymn to the tree from which the cross of Jesus was made: '*Crux fidelis, inter omnes / Abor una nobilis*: / *Nulla silva talem profert / Frone, flore germina. / Dulce lignum, dulce clavos / Dulce pondus sustenit.*' ('O Faithful Cross, noblest tree. No woodland yields such saplings, in leaf or bough or blossom. Dear the nails, and dear the timber: dear the load they bear aloft').

I was not aware that in this sadomasochistic ditty I was joyfully celebrating the heroic nails as they held dear old Jesus to the beloved cross, but really, it makes little difference. I was utterly intoxicated by almost everything during those three days. A good word, 'intoxicate', for it literally means 'to poison'. Of course, the first toxins had been administered to me long before, by the various infusions, injunctions, taboos and embargoes of my religion, but now a giddy alchemy had been triggered within me, and I was filled with an entirely surreal joy.

Had I been in Lourdes or Fatima at the time, this dementia might have launched me on the path to sainthood. But this was Ratcliffe-on-the-Wreake, north Leicestershire, and Ratcliffe-on-the-Wreake doesn't do miracles, apparitions or sainthood. And so I stood outside the front of the school that Easter Saturday morning, as parents' cars eased their way up through the bars of sunlight on the tree-lined drive. I was hoping for Mum to collect me. A love of our mothers was the overwhelming emotion amongst all teenage boys: in an emotionally continent culture, this was the one indulgence that we allowed ourselves.

I recognized our car, the Vauxhall Cresta, but there was a disturbing decisiveness about the parking. The driver's door opened, and Dad got out. He gazed at the cluster of boys, unable to see me, but I saw him all right, and the other fathers also. They were not merely far younger than him, they *seemed* so much younger. That spring day I had just turned fourteen, and Dad was sixty years and nine months old, but he looked far, far older. The boys around me sensed the recognition. 'Your granddad's come for you, Kev,' said one.

My heart sank. I can, in the present tense and with icy shame, study the moments that follow like a tailor examining a bolt of inferior cloth as I walk towards him, carrying my travelling case, deeply aware that the other boys can see this elderly man coming towards me, beaming with pride and delight. He sees my face, and he knows what my look means. He is suddenly baffled and hurt, and with the eyes, it seems, of the entire school upon my back, I go one stage further. As he bends down to kiss me on the cheek, I freeze. I know I cannot be seen to reject my father's outward affection, but there's something unmanly about being seen to be kissed by such an old man. Hurriedly, he abandons the kiss.

We get into the car, and Dad reverses back onto the tree-lined drive and eases the car slowly towards the gate, the zebra-stripes of shade rippling over us.

'I'm sorry it's me,' he says as we stop at the gates, waiting for a pause in the traffic on the Seven Hills Road. 'Mum had to finish the shopping for Easter.' Poor Dad. Poor, poor Dad. God forgive me, then and now and for ever after, but rather than declare my delight at seeing him, I accepted his apology, insincerely and unconvincingly, and most all, unguiltily, even in my post-confessional ecstasy. For no sin really seemed to attach to one's behaviour towards a father, for fathers could never really be victims, but merely authors or culprits.

I have no memory of that Easter, other than I had a row with Dad after refusing to kiss him goodnight, because, as I angrily told him, real men don't do that. Real men, of course, do. I ran up to my bedroom, and shortly afterwards, Mum came up with the message that Dad was sorry. A really decent boy would have gone downstairs to make amends. I didn't.

Leicester City had miraculously reached the FA Cup Final that year. I was excused school the Saturday morning of the match, and Dad and I went to London by train, travelling first class, with a special three-course lunch. He was clearly so proud to be with his son, attending the high point of the soccer year. Outside Wembley we were suckered into posing for a picture by a photographer with a parrot. (Did he ever get such easier dupes? Father and son, idiots alike). I am looking at the picture now: I am fourteen, the bird on my shoulder, and a clear foot shorter than Dad, meaning that I am about 4'10'. Dad is sixty, but he appears to be at least eighty. My heart fills with pity as he looks lovingly, proudly at me, through the lens and down the decades. Poor Dad. Leicester City were put to the sword, of course.

UNLIKE when my brothers had been there, Ratcliffe was now deeply philistine, and I doubt very much if any year was as philistine as mine. We had absolutely no regard for literature or art (which was entirely absent from the Ratcliffe syllabus). The only values that we esteemed were those of the rugby pitch. It is quite pitiful to think that my father was paying about one fifth of his post-tax income to give me an education that was considerably inferior to that of Wyggeston, which charged nothing. By now, I had come to know my fellow voyagers into academic mediocrity. There was John Stanley, the alpha male of my year, a Birmingham lad, superb athlete and an engaging and witty boy. He was powerful and forbidding and I would never have dared cross him. Another rugby player was Dave Ploughman, the son of a Liverpool businessman, who was tall and ungainly and bespectacled and impossible to dislike. Both he and John Stanley possessed a very English stolidity and courage. Their friend John O'Malley was the son of a Leicestershire doctor. He was unsure of himself, sometimes slightly pompous, sometimes a bit of a clown to impress John Stanley. He was not especially clever, but wholly without malice. Decent sums him up. Andrew Campbell was also a rugby forward, and even at that age was an immensely muscled youngster with a fierce rage who would break things rather than hit anyone. Bernie Kelly was another rugby player, Birmingham-Irish, unquenchably brave and very brilliant: his passion was single-celled protozoa. The only boy that I knew who was ardent about culture in any sense was Richard Burgess, whose parents were both commercial artists. Sending him to Ratcliffe was rather like vegetarians putting their boy through bullfighting school.

The dominant personality in our lives was Father Claud Leetham MA, who belonged to a common species in England: he was a patrician philistine, with a kindly manner, a booming upper-class voice and no sense whatever of the arts. He loved rugby players and loud, strong personalities. The modest, self-effacing aesthetic or ascetic was incomprehensible to him. He was a swaggering, likeable, arrogant, noisy fool, who if he knew self-doubt did so in the darker watches of the whiskey-fuelled nights to which his radiantly red nose supplied ample testimony.

He was the man behind Ratcliffe's new church, which had been designed by a Welsh architect, sculptor and rogue named Jonah Jones. He had already executed a bust of the founding father of Ratcliffe, Antonio Gentili, which now stood in the front hall. The guileful Jones had given the face the irrefutable features of Claud Leetham, but it was the boys' satirical daily stroking of the nose that had supplied the identifying mucky smear across its bridge.

The boys felt an affection for Claud, whereas they felt none whatever for his deputy, Jack Morris, a suave saurian biped with no evident feelings, affections, or humour. His face was thin and streamlined, and his irreproachable black hair was always swept back to reveal the delicate temples of an Iago. The Ratcliffe folklore was that his father had invented the zip, and he had turned his back on a fortune to become a priest. He was quite the coldest, most unfathomable man in the school; trying to get into his mind was like trying to psychoanalyse a cat. Yet there was no denying his brilliance. He specialized in English, but he could instantly turn his hand to history, or maths, or physics, or French or Latin, without any teaching aids. No real smile ever rose on his face that was not sardonic or dismissive, and no affection of any kind glowed in his eyes. He wore an ankle-length cassock, and glided silently along the school corridors as if on castors. It is hard to imagine him ever having a shit.

The head of senior school, Father Nann, was a handsome, conceited man, with greying black hair, always impeccably groomed. He was a compelling deliverer of sermons, knowing the melodramatic touches that would please boys. He enjoyed the authority of being head of senior school, and revelled in the power of the icy look. The high point of his week came on Wednesday afternoons, when he donned the uniform of the Combined Cadet Force, in which he was, I think, a captain. He wore the flat soft cap with élan, flair, éclat, panache and whatever other French words come to mind. This semi-infatuation with his own image, before an audience of mere schoolboys, provides the real insight into his deeply immature personality.

I had chosen to join the boy scouts rather than the cadets. This option had been made possible by Bert Orton, the Viennese Jew, most of whose family had perished in Hitler's gas chambers. His real name was Herbert Oppenheimer, and he and his mother had escaped before the Gestapo had come for them. A dedicated convert to Catholicism, he was easily the most brilliant member of staff, fluent of course in German and English but also French and Italian, and passably competent in half-a-dozen other languages. He was also a formidable historian, a master of the histories of most European countries and an expert in English eighteenth- and nineteenth-century history.

He had enlisted in the British army when war came, and the military bureaucracy looked at this brilliant intellectual, completely fluent in the languages of both main enemies and their main continental ally. Did they put him into intelligence, or the code-breaking operations at Bletchley? No, with true British genius, they gave him a spade and posted him to the Pioneer Corps, which specialized in digging trenches.

This experience proved to him the fatuity of military life, so he had started an alternative to the cadets, a boy-scout troop. I had illustrious precursors. Bill had been senior boy in the CCF, and David had been chief scout. But I had already been in a scout troop in Leicester, so I joined Bert Orton's group.

Bert was a good man, and Dad liked him a lot, which said a great deal, for experience had taught him to be sceptical about people. They had much in common, for both were guileless, and Bert's presence at Ratcliffe when he could have graced an Oxford or Cambridge college remains a mystery. Dad's attitude to Jews generally was tinged with some of the prejudices of his youth in which the term 'Jewman' was the colloquialism for money lender. The newspapers of his childhood would routinely identify Jews as a primary statement of identity, as in a headline 'Jew Charged

With Theft'. Dad's first surgery had been in Harrington Street, Dublin, also known as Little Palestine. The street directory even Hebraicized his name into 'Meyer', which probably didn't please him too much. He wasn't a Jew-hater – his friendship with Bert showed that – but merely a flawed man with the flaws of his time.

That time visited us unexpectedly during my first summer holiday from Ratcliffe. Bill was reading *Ulysses* (which I still haven't managed to do) when he let out a mighty roar. We all raced to him. He was shaking with excitement, his finger quivering on an open page of the green-clad book. 'It's Uncle Jack, by Jove!' Dad cried. 'Uncle Jack! And mentioned in *Ulysses*, no less!' Indeed he was, a passing aside:

> BLOOM (Rubs his hands cheerfully.) Just like old times. Poor Bloom!
>
> (Reuben J. Dodd, black bearded Iscariot, bad shepherd, bearing on his shoulders the drowned corpse of his son, approaches the pillory.)
>
> REUBEN J. (Whispers hoarsely.) The squeak is out. A split is gone for the flatties. Nip the first rattler.
>
> THE FIRE BRIGADE Pflaap!
>
> BROTHER BUZZ (Invests Bloom in a yellow habit with embroidery of painted flames and high pointed hat. He places a bag of gunpowder round his neck and hands him over to the civil power, saying.) Forgive him his trespasses.
>
> (Lieutenant Myers of the Dublin Fire Brigade by general request sets fire to Bloom. Lamentations.)
>
> THE CITIZEN Thank heaven!
>
> BLOOM (In a seamless garment marked I. H. S. stands upright amid phoenix flames.) Weep not for me, O daughters of Erin.

(He exhibits to Dublin reporters traces of burning. The daughters of Erin, in black garments with lace prayer-books and long lighted candles in their hands, kneel down and pray.)

Of course many people of James Joyce's Dublin earned a snapshot mention, but imagine – my father, finding that his beloved uncle, the man who had almost been a father to him, had been mentioned in the most famous Irish book of all time. And I have looked into Jack Myers. One of the last references to him in *The Irish Times* in the 1920s is of a wall falling on him, but fortunately his helmet had taken most of the weight of the blow. The dented helmet of that news story might today be a still-intact item in the James Joyce Museum in Dublin, had not the next generation of the Myers family, namely me, completely destroyed it.

Over the next few days Dad reminisced about his youth in Ireland, only the second time (that I recollect) he ever did. Most of his memories were fond and ruminative, as he stood with his back to the empty fireplace and spoke of that distant era when *Ulysses* was being written and he was young. He told me of the men he knew in his youth. Only one of them moved him to anger, someone called 'Lemass'. I didn't pursue the reasons for Dad's rage.

THE DORMITORY in my second year was rather more agricultural than St Joseph's. There was no running water in the washroom basins, which we filled with buckets from a cold-water tap. Perhaps a regimen of ice-cold water was intended to stifle the emergence of sexual desire, which in my case wasn't necessary. Physically I was still a small boy. Three years younger than me, my brother Johnny's voice had broken when he was no more than twelve. At the wedding of my sister Ann to an old Ratcliffian, Michael Hinchliffe, he had gone round with slightly but nonetheless nobly bent knees in order to conceal the truth that he was already taller than me. But there he is, all these years later in the treacherous wedding pictures of the day, stooping there, generously bi-genuflecting.

Most of my dormitory were reluctant to get out of bed immediately after the wake-up call, and would wait for several minutes to allow their morning erections to shrivel and die of their own accord – all, that is, save one boy called Davis, who would stride off to the washroom with his penis sturdily to the fore against the taut fabric of his pyjamas, like a foremast raking around Cape Horn.

In May, when I had just turned fifteen, I was one of a group of scouts on a weekend camp near a village called Shepshed, a few miles away. On our second afternoon, Richard Burgess, Andrew Campbell and I went for a walk. We came to a woodland grove, glowing greenly in the late spring sunlight, with a lush carpet of wildflowers beneath our feet. In the heart of the wood lay a hill, on the top of which stood a ruined statue to Venus. The slopes were covered in flowering rhododendron and azalea bushes, in tiered banks of purple, maroon and vermilion, and around our feet lay a sea of bluebells. It was such a beautiful place that the three of us were struck speechless for several minutes, before Richard spoke. 'This makes me see why there must be a God.'

Me: 'This makes me see why I could become a priest.'

Andrew: 'This makes me see that I am not worthy to become a priest.'

Nauseating, but a useful indicator of the piety that filled our daily lives. Boys back from their Christmas holidays would even proudly show one another the hand-carved rosary beads they'd just been given as presents. We might discuss liturgy and engine blocks in the same breath. Andrew Campbell – who was ardent about religion and cars; Richard Burgess called him our resident Cartholic – told me of the forthcoming Ford range of saloons, with new engines and gear boxes. The whole project would make the current Ford range immediately obsolete. I made a note to tell Dad.

I was still a daily communicant, though more reluctantly, not least because Mass no longer felt quite the same. The Latin rite had been replaced by an English liturgy of surpassing banality. Moreover, Pugin's glorious Victorian church had been both deconsecrated and then vandalized into classrooms, its place now taken by Jonah Jones' garish new building. Though modernism usually prided itself on function over form, this church managed to get neither right. One of its design flaws was that large numbers of bluebottles would roost in dark and companiable clusters within the blue-ceilinged dome above us. During Mass, however, the rising warmth of the congregation would cause the ceiling's residents to lose their grip, and High Mass would be enlivened by a rainfall of tumbling bodies, and the crunching sound of their being disposed of.

One Sunday morning I was going home for the day, hoping Mum would collect me. As I stood at the school front door, my heart again sank when I saw Dad emerge slowly from the gathering of parked cars, a strange smile on his face. I sauntered over to him and shook his hand, then looked round for the familiar Cresta.

'Where's the car, Dad?'

He gestured proudly at the vehicle beside him – it was a new car, a Ford Zodiac, but of the newly obsolete variety. He stood there, looking so happy, and to add to my mortification, I saw he was wearing leather bedroom slippers. I got in. The door didn't close properly, even though it was new. I had to struggle to lock it.

'The dealer said the hinges will settle down in time – all new Fords are like that.'

'Dad, why did you buy this?'

'Well, it was time for a new one, and you'd told me about the Zodiac …'

No! Not this one! I shrieked inwardly – the one that's going to replace it! Though I said nothing, ruthless silence before such evident pride was as pointed as explicit disapproval. Fresh surprises awaited me at home. My uncle Ted (Dad's brother-in-law) in Dublin had recently died, bequeathing Dad a small hand-carved ebony Indian elephant. Dad had made a rubber mould from it, and then created a dozen appalling parodies, with thick, coarse trunks – and because the mould had failed to capture small details, he had then painted the eyes on. These horrors were now dotted throughout the sitting and dining-rooms. I lifted one up. Dad looked at me expectantly. I said nothing.

We again went on holidays to Criccieth, in Dad's new Ford, which I hated, though at least his melancholia seemed to have stabilized. One evening he drove the family to the Goat Inn in Baedgelert, and in recognition of my advancing years, bought me a lager and lime. I found the flavour of alcohol disgusting, and didn't touch it again for years. He drank a pint of Guinness and smoked a couple of Number 6 cigarettes, which for health reasons he had taken up in preference to the untipped Churchman or Gold Flake of my childhood.

Each day we went to Blackrock beach, to gaze at sand and dune and a flat grey sea. A couple from Leicester whom we half knew chanced across Mum and Dad. A conversation followed. Bored, I retreated to the dunes to read my book, half-listening to the voices a few yards away. The sound of further greetings. Then rustling through the grass. I looked up. The couple's daughter appeared before me, sheltered from my family by one dune, and from me, feet away, by another. Unaware of my presence, she began to get changed. Within a moment, a naked girl stood before me. She was blonde, fifteen and impossibly beautiful. I gazed in utter awe at this sumptuous she-youth, with her slender hips and her long legs: could pubic hair be so fair, labia so delicate, buttocks so fine, breasts so conical? She looked this way and that, presumably fearing an intruder, not knowing that here the intruder was she. I was not especially aroused, more entranced at this vision of perfect beauty. She got into her costume, never knowing she had a witness of her every movement.

Sex was also arriving in the larger world. The first James Bond movie, *Doctor No*, was released, and apparently, Bond clearly did it with girls. The whole thing. With lots of them. No one had ever painted such a cinematic view of sexually active unmarried manhood that was available to teenagers. After a hockey match in Nottingham, some of the XV were invited to take tea with an Old Ratcliffian called Maurice Beamish, but he had been suddenly called out on business, so we sat talking to his wife Mary, with our cake and sandwiches awkwardly perched on our knees.

'Have any of you seen this new Bond film?' she asked. She was in her early thirties and had an unusual amount of cleavage for a Saturday afternoon. 'I hear it's very sexy. Have you ever seen a sexy film, Kevin?'

'No, Mrs Beamish, I haven't.'

'You should. I think you'd like something that's really sexy. I certainly do. Everyone does. Bet they don't tell you that in Ratcliffe, do they?'

'No, Mrs Beamish.'

She looked me in the eye and touched me on the knee and smiled. In the hall, the other boys shook her hand, and turned away. She lightly kissed my fifteen-year-old lips, and then the vixen steered me through her front door, as I felt the surge of real sexual desire for the very first time.

I had joined the Astronomy Society, which was run by the most eccentric member of the community, Brother Primavesi. Despite his name, Prim was the very embodiment of Englishness. A botanist and bee-keeper, he collected animal skulls the way that others might have hoarded pornography or stamps, and was also a regular tourist into outer space. The arrival of winter's dark nights made telescopic journeys into the solar system possible, and one day Brother Primavesi announced that the auspices for that evening were good: with luck, we should be able to see Saturn and its rings, and we were to wrap up well. After supper, we gathered outside Prim's room, and decked out in a weird woollen cap and a flea-infested overcoat that he had apparently stolen from the frozen body of a dead tramp, he led us up Ratcliffe's bell tower, high over the school, high over the valleys of the rivers Wreake and Soar and the north Leicestershire wolds.

'Gentlemen,' he whispered in the moonless dark, 'looking east, there's no higher point than here until you reach the Urals. That's it. You are above everything in Europe.'

Primavesi could well have been right, though we could see nothing, perched so high on this cold bare night: ink black below, ink-black around, a starry, moonless, ink-black above. But an imagined line of sight eastward from that bell tower would have run over the fields of Leicestershire, the pastures of Rutland, the soke of Peterborough and the Great Fens and the plains of Norfolk till it made seafall, east of Acle and north of Great Yarmouth, and thence over the even greater plains of the North Sea, until landfall near the Horn of Holland. Our unseeing gaze would have travelled through the dark over the polders of the Netherlands to the flatlands of Low Germany to Berlin, which that mythic Ratcliffian had perished trying to bomb, and onward to Poland and the wide lands of the Vistula, before passing above Belorussia and northern Ukraine. I think now that we might have been halted by the Central Russian Upland, but maybe Prim had found a valley down which our hypothetical gaze could safely travel before breaking onto the steppes, and thereafter, all the way to the Urals. Somewhere beyond that mountain range, I knew, lay the Soviet missile bases, which were pointing their weaponry west, and some of their targets now lay just before me, mere miles away. The V bombers and Thor missiles stood on their runways and their launch pads at RAF Bruntingthorpe and RAF Cottesmore, not far from where our imaginary transcontinental journey had begun. Prim pointed the telescope upwards, and by the druidical processes of divination known only to astronomers found a point in the sky that, sure enough, turned out to be Saturn. One by one in that cold tower we studied it, gazing at the thinly glowing rings, as precise as if on a cut-glass ornament, before it was time for bed.

At around the same time as my visit to the bell tower a U2 spyplane flew over Cuba and confirmed that the USSR was building a ballistic missile base there. President Kennedy announced a blockade of the island. Suddenly we were on the brink of nuclear war: there still has never been such a grave crisis. We boys abandoned the pop music of Radio Luxembourg and listened instead to the American Forces Network. The school was called together each evening to pray for peace, and as tension mounted, the atmosphere grew more fervent. We were all aware that if war started, the nearness of the RAF bases meant that we should inevitably be caught by the nuclear inferno of the first exchanges. Boys queued to say emotional farewells to their parents from the single phone kiosk available to us until Father Nann ended any further melodramatic and sometimes tearful conversations by simply and sensibly disconnecting the phone.

As the crisis intensified, one evening we heard that an American task force would, over the coming hours, be intercepting a Russian missile convoy somewhere in the Atlantic – and on that satisfyingly terrifying note, we retired to our dormitories to discuss our imminent fate. We all knew that death, if it came, would not be instant, as in the centre of Hiroshima, but slowly and terribly, by our being blinded and burnt, as in its outskirts. The problem was, would we sleep?

We slept. Sometime in the middle of the night, the school siren sounded, for the first time ever, waking us all with shocking suddenness. 'Christ, it's war,' said a voice in the dark.

We were struggling out of bed when Brother Atkins put his head in the door. He was in a dressing-gown.

'Move, gentlemen, if you please,' he said. 'This is not a drill. This is the real thing. Walk slowly to the assembly hall. Do not run. Do not panic. Good luck.'

We put on our dressing-gowns and with granite-coloured faces went downstairs, along the corridors already full of gowned boys shuffling in slapping slippers across the marble floor. I found myself beside one of the doughty Gallagher brothers: he was silently lip-saying the rosary, his beads in his hand. At the end of the corridor, we left the main building into the open air, and towards the gymnasium.

'The RAF's been scrambled,' said a voice.

'The Russians've bombed New York,' said another.

I gazed east. The missiles would be arriving any second now. I briefly wondered if I would see them coming in, but then dismissed that idea. I would see nothing. My eyes would be melted by the flash. I didn't pray to be spared – survival was simply not possible. I merely prayed that I should die instantly. I thought of my parents and family in Medina Road, soon too die also, just over the horizon. I would never see them again.

In the assembly hall, we were formed into our classes, and prefects began to read out the names of class members: Adcock, here, Browne, here, Coughlan, here, Donovan, here, Downes, here, in calm, clipped tones. It was a perfect essay in English stiff-upper-lipdom by boys whose grandparents probably hailed from Ballina and Bohola, as we calmly but fearfully awaited death. There was no panic and no tears. Resigned and stoic, we were resolved. We should all die like good little Englishmen.

Then a senior priest, Father 'Beetle' Moss, came in, and mounted the stage. Silence fell. Beetle blinked owlishly at us through his bottle-end glasses, and struggled for words.

'Christ. London must've copped it,' someone whispered.

In that moment death seemed to stride into the hall.

Beetle finally managed to find his voice. Clearing his throat, he apologized for the inconvenience, and then proceeded to deliver some quite appalling news. We were not, after all, going to die. There had been a fire in the school, caused by a leak under an oil tank, but it was now under control, and in a few minutes we could all return to our dormitories. How *unfair*.

So, there we all were, just having been mercilessly snatched from the jaws of a thermonuclear holocaust, mundanely traipsing back to our dormitories, with years, decades even, ahead of us.

One of the boys in our dormitory was a very tall, handsome lad by the name of Paul Chatfield, whose preposterously beautiful mother seemed barely older than us. Only a couple of days after the tragically unfulfilled nuclear threat, Paul burst into the dormitory. 'Have you heard this new band? It's hilarious! They're called the Beetles. Like Beetle Moss!'

Beetle Moss, the hero of the Cuban missile crisis, had a braying laugh, which people always imitated whenever his name was mentioned. We all brayed together. What a mad name! And how long could such a group last? Within a couple of days, we'd all heard 'Love Me Do'. I say this without wisdom-in-hindsight – but we all knew that we were hearing something wholly new and unique. 'The Beatles' (as we discovered the name was spelt) had a strange sound that somehow spoke to the teenage soul. It was exotic and visceral, and in some mysterious way related to seeing the Sand Hill Girls squat and wee, or the strange, uncomfortably sweet feelings when Mrs Campbell kissed me.

That single fortnight, with the James Bond film officially authorizing sexual licence, the Cuban Missile Crisis and the release of the Beatles' first single, provided one of the cultural watersheds of the twentieth century. This itself was made possible by the refusal of the military and political elites of the USA and the USSR, both of whom had gone through the Second World War, to allow themselves to be slaves either to treaty or technology. Simultaneously, I suspect that a vast teenage subconscious decided that it was time to walk away from the twentieth century's valleys of death, to the sunlit uplands of music and love and personal freedom. That I remember these days so clearly suggests that more than a lively adolescent imagination was at work. A quite new and different generation was being shaped.

Eleven

DAD COLLECTED me at the end of the first term in the fifth form, in the wretched Ford. Again he noticed my disappointment that it was him, not Mum, and again he apologized. I made no attempt to hide my irritation with him. Yet relations were still good enough for him to ask me to accompany him to see Mr Thom in a geriatric hospital. He wasn't that old in years, in his early sixties perhaps, but a withered Methuselah lay in the bed. His eyes were vacant as he babbled aimlessly, his thin hands faltering over the edge of the sheet. His features were strangely beaked, his nose like a quill.

'That's the last time you'll see him,' said Dad as we walked back to the Ford. 'He's finished.'

'How do you know?'

'Did you see how sharp his chin and nose were? A sure sign of impending death.'

The words of the Hostess in *Henry V* came back to me: '... for after I saw him fumble with the sheets, and play with flowers, and smile upon his fingers' end, I knew there was but one way; for his nose was as sharp as a pen.' I quoted the lines to Dad, and he looked at me with a visible approval that was not to last.

I had found a corner of the dining-room where the family's single transistor radio could just about pick up Radio Éireann, to which I would listen wonderingly as if the mysteries of Irish traditional music were confided to me alone.

'What are you doing?' asked Dad, seeing me with my ear to the radio.

'Listening to Radio Éireann!' I replied, delighted at my receptive antennae.

He looked at me sadly. 'Hmp. Fat lot of good that'll do you.'

The front doorbell rang while we were at Christmas dinner a couple of days later. It was Mrs Thom, more haggard than ever. 'I'm sorry for disturbing you,' she said, 'but I thought I should tell you. Mr Thompson passed away this morning. Now please get on with your Christmas Day. There's nothing any of you can do for me.' She turned and departed into the dark afternoon, a gaunt grey raven, to attend to her first few hours of widowhood, in yuletide solitude.

The next day, Boxing Day, snow started to fall, as was the yearly pattern in Leicester. This time, however, it was different. It didn't just snow for a couple of hours, but non-stop through the day and the following night, and the day after. A unique weather system had arrived. An anticyclone over Scandinavia had inhaled frozen air from Siberia and exported it to Britain, while a high pressure area over Iceland blocked the usual mild wet breezes from the Atlantic, The cliché of being in the grip of a vice really did apply, as the cold steel of the Arctic closed in on two fronts, meeting in Britain. Whenever the blizzards ceased, a hard frost followed. All of Leicester was covered in a thick coating of hard-baked snow. So too was England. The greatest freeze of the twentieth century was underway.

We couldn't attend Mr Thompson's funeral, so presumably his cadaver vanished into the frozen clay, leaving poor Mrs Thom alone and unseen in her icebound graveside vigil. The day that I was meant to return to Ratcliffe, I began to clear the snow around the car. A steel sheet of iron lay on the windscreen, so I got the keys from Mum and turned on the engine, and the internal heater. After a couple of minutes, it was clear that the heater in this 'new' Ford didn't work. I was fifteen, and now had a point to prove. I went back into the house, to the surgery, where Dad was working.

'The car heater's broken,' I said, crossly.

'Worse things have happened.'

'Why did you get that bloody car?'

'Because it was time, and you suggested we get a Ford.'

'But not that one.'

'Don't talk to me like that.'

'Why do you always get things wrong? Always. You've got those ridiculous bloody elephants everywhere. We've had a half-finished coal bunker for about ten years. Other fathers aren't like you. They get things right.'

'Well I'm sorry that I'm not like other fathers, but maybe they haven't had my health problems.'

'Yes, you and your health problems, and that so-called weak heart of yours.'

At which point, Dad rose from behind his desk and hit me across the face with his open hand. I fell back, into the hall. He then kicked me across the floor, through the open door into the sitting room, where I ended up, curled in a protective huddle. His feet, as usual, were slippered, and the kicks didn't really hurt me. With the wisdom of years, I can confidently declare that I fully deserved everything I got, and more. As he walked away, I picked myself up, went to my bedroom, collected my suitcase, and went downstairs. Mum had been working in the kitchen, and had been entirely unaware of what had happened, and would remain so, to her death twenty-eight years later.

'Have you said goodbye to Daddy?' she asked.

'Yes,' I lied.

We walked out of the kitchen door, along the path through the snow that I'd swept clear that morning. I now had to scrape the fresh coat of icing from the windscreen. I merely managed to make a hole in the sheet. Peering through this small aperture, Mum drove carefully down Buckminster Road, onto Blackbird Road, and then out towards the Loughborough Road. The entire countryside outsidse the city shimmered white, but I was too angry with Dad, and too upset at leaving Mum, to pay much attention. She was so focussed on driving that she couldn't wipe the mist from the windscreen, so I sat forward, repeatedly clearing it with my gloved hand.

Ratcliffe was frozen through to its heart, its central heating in this Arctic embrace as futile as Mrs Partington's mop, even without the generous contributions from oaken doors that didn't close properly, and the leaded windows, which simply served as heat extractors. The school was also cold in another dimension. The bumbling Claud Leetham had been overthrown in a palace coup by that austere and glacial reptile Jack Morris. What a contest that must have been – Machiavelli versus Micawber. Morris took the first assembly of the new term in saturnine triumph, his polished temples pale and serene in the ice-cold air. He unashamedly announced a change in direction for the school, and then swept out of the gym, like a dark spectre gliding over the pack ice.

OVER THE COMING DAYS snow continued to fall on the rolling hills of north Leicestershire, and each night, refroze, as if nature was diligently laying down an ice age's archaeological history. All outdoor games were now impossible – not just here, but everywhere across the length and breadth of Britain. The entire island was a sports-free glacier, but with a single green footprint at its very centre: Leicester City's Filbert Street ground. The previous summer, an unusually far-seeing management had installed under-pitch heating and so Leicester was able to play its night-time FA Cup Match against Ipswich Town on the last

Wednesday in January. Before I went up to the dormitory, I got the result on the radio: 3-1 to Leicester: Ken Keyworth scoring twice. As I got ready for bed, Paul Chatfield was enthusing about The Beatles' latest record, 'Please Please Me'. It was so cool.

Some hours into the night, a hand on my shoulder bestirred me from the deep. 'Wake up,' a voice was saying. 'Wake up, Kevin.'

'What ... what?' I blinked awake, wondering if this time we were really at war. It was Beetle Moss. He had a torch.

'Get dressed. Your father's been taken ill. His partner is coming to collect you.'

'His partner? Dr Ludwig?'

'That's the fellow. Don't wake the others. Get dressed by this,' and he gave me a torch. 'And bring your coat. It's cold.'

I dressed hurriedly, and I found him downstairs, waiting. He escorted me to the front door, his cassock echoing loudly through the soundless corridor of a totally silent school: swish swish swish. The dark air lay cold and thick around us, like pond water. We reached the wooden settle beside the oak front door and sat there for an age, until we saw the approaching headlights from the driveway crossing the ceiling in strange shifting rectangles, before swivelling enquiringly through the windows beside the door, then coming to a halt. We walked outside, and the wind hit me with a shovel.

Sbish Ludwig was in a new Rover with a walnut fascia. Ah, even this Polish exile had outclassed poor Dad. Beetle Moss opened the car door for me, and then he went round to Sbish and exchanged a few words with him before returning to my side.

'Good luck Kevin,' he then said, patting me on the shoulder through the still-open door. 'I'll pray for you and your father tonight, and tomorrow at Mass.'

'Thank you, Father, but I'm sure it'll be fine.'

Inwardly, I scolded Dad and his imagination. Sbish said nothing in that long, slow, cold journey through the heaped snow banks that lined the Seven Hills Road into Leicester. I could hear the car clock above the silken purring of the Rover engine: tock … tock … tock.

Sbish dropped me off at Medina Road and left for the hospital. Maggy and Johnny and Ann were there, but Mum too was at the hospital.

'Dad and his heart,' I jeered softly, 'yet again.'

I looked around, expecting little smiles at my jest.

'You don't understand,' said Ann. 'You wouldn't have been brought from Ratcliffe if it wasn't serious.'

'But it's not that serious,' I protested. 'I mean, we'd know, wouldn't we, if it was that serious. Sbish would have said something.'

I asked Johnny how his new sledge was going. He'd been given it for his thirteenth birthday, the week before. Finally, we had our own sledge, but the snowfall had been far too heavy for Johnny to use it. So we sat and waited. I spoke occasionally, about Dad, and his bloody hypochondria. So stupid, getting me out of school for nothing. And next morning I'd have to go back. I was sitting, haunches perched on the grey, leather-covered horizontal-facing coal scuttle when Mum finally appeared at the sitting-room door. I felt a smile rise to my face. Panic over. Phew.

SHE SAID, 'Daddy's gone.'

SOMEWHERE inside my memory cells reside the designated molecules that hold the secrets to the horror of the week that followed. I have often gone looking for those molecules, to discover what events they might reveal, but have never found them. What I remember now is what I remembered ten years ago and twenty years ago and probably a month after the catastrophe had occurred. Almost nothing.

Feelings, however, remain: for the very worst, the most evil and unspeakable feeling in my entire life came when I woke in a frozen bed next morning, and realized that Dad was dead. Gone forever. And I hadn't said goodbye to him, hadn't wished him well, but instead had mocked him and provoked him into hitting me, and then had turned my back on him, not for that day, but for all time.

I do not write this lightly now. Grief is like a glittering diamond, the way it endures and the way it cuts, long after the departure of the white-hot, tectonic pressures of guilt and loss that forged it from the human carbon of ordinary life. There is no known solvent for that bitter gem, save time, but of all the exquisite edges with which grief can lacerate, none compares with the glittering imperishable shard that is guilt.

Perhaps only Catholics can understand what I am talking about. For who or what did I not feel guilt about? There was poor Mum, a widow with three children of school age and desolation all around her. And there was Johnny, with his precious virgin sledge, the Rosebud that was in fact never to be used, his childhood slain in a winter's hour. And there was Maggy, who would now have to mind Mum when I returned to school. But most of all, the key to everything, the missile launched from its silo: Dad had died of a heart attack, precisely as he had long feared, and for which obsession I had mercilessly mocked him down the years.

People arrived from Ireland and slept everywhere. I cannot tell you much more. But I remember the Requiem Mass in a freezing cold St Peter's Church, the black vestments, the black candles guttering in the cold and dark as the Rosminian Choir, who had journeyed from Ratcliffe, once again incanted the dirge of death: '*Dies Irae / Dies Illa / Solvet saeclum in favilla / Tested David cum Sybilla*'. When I had first heard those words two years before, I was in a state of spiritual ecstasy. Now I was in a trance of disbelieving misery. I was an altar boy for the day, a mere supernumerary doing a few menial liturgical tasks out of filial duty. Sobs shook the church. The adult male choir lowed in the cold grey shadows. The congregation of heavy serge overcoats rose and sank as the rites of a final Mass unfolded, and a man's obsequies were tersely intoned.

Next, we were standing on the tundra of Gilroes Cemetery, beside a coffin-shaped hole in the frozen Groby loam. The snow came in swirling flusters out of an iron-grey ceiling a few feet above our heads. Brief funereal verses were swept away on the northern wind, while Mum wept. We all wept, discreetly, bravely, warm trickles down cheeks sculpted from the sheet-ice of our flesh. Then the coffin was lowered through the heavy marl that overnight sturdy men had broken open with spades. This was it. The shocking realization, yes, this was it. This was your father you were burying. Forever.

A day of burial is a day of birth. A new posthumous existence is born beside the grave, from fragments looted from the old regime, and reassembled over the coming days. But things do not fit. The missing bits are gone completely. We must improvise for this new life of ours, for it must be made up of cannibalized parts. Jigsaw pieces now lack their familiar neighbours, so they must be cut or hammered into place. That's it. That's life after bereavement.

We had just returned to Medina Road when the phone rang. It was Jack Morris. I was to come back to Ratcliffe that evening.

'I can't, sir. There's no one to drive me.'

'Come come, Myers, I'm sorry, but that is simply not good enough. All right, you've got away with it today. But you're to be in my office at 11 am tomorrow. I don't want you using your father's funeral to dodge any more lessons.'

Someone drove me to school next morning, I have no idea who, and Morris saw me in his office. His face was darker and smoother than ever before, his lips more lean and purposeful and his hands were folded before him, pale, manicured and unmoving, like those of a dead concert pianist in his coffin. I don't think he had a clue what bereavement was, or love, or loss of any kind. He was the undead debris from the train crash of his life, now following its own smooth and heartless trajectory. I say that now – such wisdom was not allowed me then. I stood before him, broken and forlorn, as he spoke in cold clipped words. I was to return to my studies, and I was not to use this 'tragedy' (he intoned the dissociative inverted commas as if he were speaking some distasteful rock 'n' roll neologism) to avoid my duties. He had his eye on me.

I realized then that he really disliked me. He told me to go immediately to my class. I knew where: additional maths, in a special room set aside for the handful who had embarked on the depraved parabola of calculus, sine, cosine and the boundless delinquencies of integers. There was silence as I entered. I took my seat.

'Well done, Myers, that's the spirit,' said my teacher, and continued teaching. A hand touched my shoulder. That was pretty much it, save for a kindly Indian student named Diaz, whom I barely knew and who spoke to me after class. He took my hand in both of his, nearly weeping in sympathy.

Thus was the rest of my life born in that sorry Arctic season when the world was ice and I was fifteen. There are no words for the silent tumults that lie beneath the outward shallows of the teenage boy. Profundity and callowness swirl around one another, like the waters of a warm river entering a freezing sea. The feelings are too inchoate for words, and the emotions too unshaped to merit definition. But the core of all this was simple. It was love.

A child's love for his parent doesn't measure worldly skills with rule and scales, but returns what is given, even if only in faltering and inadequate measure. For during every second of my life my father had loved me, and he had always shown it. We often use the word 'love' as if it is a single thing, but it is not: for the human heart is an ark of love, housing an entire menagerie of creatures of affection. Each kind of love behaves differently. Romantic love arrives like cavalry on a plain, with trumpets and banners. The love for a mother is deep and respected and esteemed in all cultures. Sibling love is nurtured in the nursery, and fed on scraps and fights and feuds, both with one another, and together against the outside world. A little boy's love for his father is dependent and awed and is in perpetual receipt. But a teenage boy's love for his father lies like a slumbering whale, deep beneath the surface of an angry sea. I did not show my love because I didn't even know it was there. For all his ineptitude, and the tragedy that had defined his life, I had really loved poor Dad.

I brainlessly immersed myself in pop music and studies, and soon a games master, Brother O'Dwyer, decided that games must resume before the incarcerated boys went stir-crazy. So tractors and rollers were brought out, and the snow was ground into packed flat ice to make a playing surface that was hard, lethal and level. In those days, hockey goalkeepers did battle with just shin pads on their legs and a box on their groin, but no face mask, no helmet, and no chest or stomach armour: if you were hit on the face, you got a new face. Since almost no one wanted to be goalkeeper (and true to my mythic sense of Irishness) I volunteered to play there. I discovered I was quite good. Though my voice still hadn't broken, I was chosen for the Third XI, composed mostly of boys who were several inches taller than me. The captain was Richard Brucciani, a Leicester lad of Italian ancestry, and a remarkably fine young gentleman and natural leader. Incredibly, I even found a sort of happiness on the hockey icefields during that endless winter.

Though he had feared a heart attack for many years, with a classically Hibernian improvidence, Dad had died intestate. His bank account was frozen, while Mum didn't even have an account of her own, and credit cards did not then exist. She was therefore completely penniless. (Her friend Kathy Black had been widowed when her husband Alec, also a GP, had been killed driving in fog on the Seven Hills Road the year before. The British Medical Association had promptly paid her £200 in cash to help her cope with sudden expenses. But Alec had been Scottish Presbyterian and a Freemason and so the BMA came to the rescue of his widow.

Dad was an Irish Catholic and not a Freemason, and naturally, the BMA did nothing for the widow of such a lesser species.) So just days after Mum had returned from the funeral, she had had to take in paying guests. She applied to Leicester Education Committee for a hardship grant to cover my school fees. The committee allowed her 80 per cent. Jack Morris insisted she find the other 20 per cent herself.

One grey afternoon, bereft, I went for a walk on the wide acres around Ratcliffe, up to the old airfield, over which, according to that Ratcliffian legend, an already dead pilot had once circled his plane, futilely signalling for help. It was now a windswept tundra, still untouched by iron roller or human foot, its rough surface of frosted snow broken by sharp clusters of frozen tussock grass, which stood like long shards of broken bottle. I didn't have proper boots, just my school shoes, and they sank deep into the snow, making my feet as cold as the ice field itself. Feet have memories, you know, and mine told me that they had twice before known cold like this. Once when Dad had taken me on the journey to Old John in Bradgate Park when I was an infant, and next when he had brought me to buy the Biggles book, just six years before. On the old snow-covered airfield, and bitten by a wind of a thousand knives, I knew total solitude, just like that poor pilot, marooned and still circling for ever. A vast hole had appeared within me, and would not go away: it wasn't just Dad that was gone. So too was certainty, and tranquillity. A bereaved family is like a suddenly blinded audience trying to leave the theatre, feeling for exits, their eyes searching for a light that will never return.

Soon afterwards, Uncle Harry, my mother's brilliantly funny, hopelessly alcoholic brother, and the link between my parents, died suddenly in Wicklow. Little else of the time remains in my mind. I scan the online archive for the music charts for that summer, but though I clearly remember the tunes, few associated memories are evoked. For the music existed in a different and desensitized plane: while my heart lay wounded on its Arctic hill, my brain still registered the sounds of a popular culture that was changing for all time. The hits of the previous five months had been by the old school of crooners and early rock 'n' roll: Elvis, Frank Ifield, Cliff Richard and the Shadows, and so on. From March of 1963 onwards, our music was all Merseyside, predominantly The Beatles, from 'Please Please Me' to 'From Me To You' and 'She Loves You', followed by the various tracks from their first album, which (I now know) was recorded the week of Dad's funeral.

But in that long season of general amnesia, two memories stand out, and both were to do with scouts, where Brother 'Peedum' Smith (he'd once sported a Parting Down the Middle, PDM) was now in charge. Early one Saturday morning in May Peedum dropped me and another scout at the village of Willoughby-on-the-Wolds, and instructed us to head for Frisby-on-the-Wreake, where a letter awaited us at a shop. This, we duly discovered, told us to go to a kitchen and an optician at the same time, and then to Belgium and Russia, all in just two days. Ah yes, this was Peedum at his capers. We solved his riddles easily enough. We stopped near the hamlet of Saxelby, and asked a farmer if we could camp on his farm. As farmers always did, he said yes. We erected our tent, cut a square in the soil nearby and removed the turf, and then built a fire and cooked some dinner. We were in our sleeping bags on the rough ground by nine, and instantly asleep. We woke at six, and having urged the embers from the night back to life, made porridge and tea. Then we put out the campfire, scattered the ashes, and put the square of turf back where the fire had been. We hoiked our rucksacks onto our backs, and leaving the campsite as perfect as if we'd never been there, trudged off through that glorious May morning. There was no human sound, just the heady songs of birds in the trees and in the hedgerows, and the skylarks calling from high above in the early morning light. We didn't speak. A strange peace filled my soul as the day warmed and the insects hummed. We went through a hamlet called Eye Kettleby, and headed for a crossroads called John O'Gaunt, which is another way of saying John of Ghent, and now we were about to finish at a place called Moscow Farm. We had got all the clues, and I felt triumphant.

We began to walk back towards Ratcliffe. We breasted a rise, and found ourselves atop a long spring-green ridge, overlooking three distinct folds in the hill system. Each little dell enclosed a village, and all three sat roughly equidistant from me, as if they were at the sunken corners of a sideless triangle. From each, a church steeple rose from amidst a cluster of ancient cottages. And as I gazed down at this most perfect image of England, the sextons duly did their filmic duty and began to ring the church bells. The chimes, gently different in time and timbre, rolled up the hills to gather round me, a threefold Sabbath melody upon this day in May, while skylarks added a fourth heavenly dimension. No other moment in my life had been so perfectly composed and so utterly beautiful. I was consummately and acutely happy, with Dad's death and all its terrible consequences, for those moments anyway, banished completely from my mind.

Three weeks later I went on another scout trip, back to the site of that yet earlier religious ecstasy the year before, at Shepshed. I was now leader of the Kestrel patrol, but solely for reasons of age, and certainly not leadership ability. I had already confirmed what I already suspected, that I completely lacked any natural authority. So before leaving for the camp, I decided on an initiative that would deeply impress the Kestrel patrol. Peedum took me aside after the scout van had been unloaded and the tent erected, clearly worried about my abilities to run things. As always, he spoke with a slightly amused air of languid authority.

'Relax, and things will be fine,' he smiled. 'But remember, you're in charge. You're responsible for all the boys here, their morals as well as everything else. Not that I expect much a problem in that department. So be a good fellow, and try not to end the weekend with too many dead bodies.' He left soon afterwards, with a wry, 'Good luck.'

Once he was gone, I announced my little triumph. I had brought a radio. Though radios were strictly contraband at Ratcliffe, a boy named Richard Taylor had one, and I borrowed it. That was how I intended to keep the Kestrel patrol happy. And so, while they listened to music, I found it easier to do the necessary tasks around the site by myself, for to ask anyone and expect obedience was merely to issue instructions to the moon. We listened to Radio Luxembourg that night by the campfire: 'Wonderful Land' by The Shadows, 'Nut Rocker' by Bee Bumble and the Stingers, and 'All Alone Am I' by the Brenda Lee. Then sleep.

As I got dressed the next morning, one of the scouts, Nigel Bates, still in his sleeping bag, gazed at me and emitted a hideous teenage cackle. 'Look! He hasn't even got any bloody hair in his armpits,' he scoffed, before turning over and going back to sleep. And so the wise lads of the Kestrel patrol slumbered on in their sleeping bags, while their poor helpless leader went out and lit the fire. It was about seven on a Sunday morning. We'd be packing up around five. Ten hours to go. I went for a walk to the rhododendron and bluebell grove beside the shrine to Venus, which had inspired such awed and imbecilic observations a year before and a lifetime ago.

When I returned to camp, I found Bates looking at a girlie magazine and showing it to other boys, who were ogling it and giggling. I had never actually seen any photographs of naked women before, and I was instantly out of my depth. Instead of ignoring it, I panicked. 'Let me see that, please.'

Smirking, Bates passed me the magazine. I opened it. Page after page of pictures of nude female flesh. *But remember, you're in charge. You're responsible for all the boys here, their morals as well as everything else.*

'I'm afraid I can't let you keep this,' I announced, throwing it into the campfire. I instantly knew I was making a catastrophic mistake as a disbelieving silence attended and the cackling flames devoured the magazine.

'Sorry,' I said. 'Orders.'

An air of a studied, toxic contempt settled over the campsite. I knew now what it was to be a prig: not strong but weak, a poor creature out of his depth, and lacking the modicum of wisdom that would take safely him to shore. I stirred the fire. No one spoke to me.

Finally Peedum arrived in the van, and we started packing in the silent, purposeful way of all people anxious to end an utterly shitty weekend. Just as we were about to leave, I realized I didn't have the radio. I unpacked my bag. No sign. I rechecked the campsite. Not a trace. This was serious, for transistors in those days were incredibly expensive. I reckoned that I could trust good old Peedum, so I told him the radio was missing.

'Hmm,' he murmured, presciently. 'That's bad.'

He ordered for the site to be searched thoroughly, and when nothing was found, for all the boys to empty their rucksacks, again to no avail. Sometimes the heart learns things before the brain, and my heart quietly told me that the theft hadn't been to acquire anything, but to inflict revenge. I was sitting beside Peedum as he drove back to school. 'A bit of a mystery about the radio. Yours, was it?'

'No, sir. Borrowed. And actually, not so much a mystery.' I explained the episode with the magazine.

He shook his head. 'You shouldn't have burnt it,' he said. 'I'd have had to have seen how bad it was. Whose was it?'

'I can't tell you, sir.' Neither a snitch nor a lick ever be.

'And the radio was stolen in revenge?'

'Yes sir.'

'A bit of a mess.'

'Yes sir.'

A bit of mess it was. The radio cost £10, or around €500 in 2016 prices, which would have been a lot of money even when Dad was alive. But it was an utter fortune now. I broke the bad news to Richard Taylor, promising him that I would repay him for it, but I needed time. He accepted that. I had given my word. That was enough.

O Levels followed thereafter. I sat ten, and, sustained by the momentum of my pre-mortem studies, got As in most subjects. Although I had been stronger by far in the arts, winning prizes in them every year, I decided that summer to do physics, chemistry and biology at A Level. It was simple, for fate and guilt agreed. I was going to follow on where poor Dad had left off. I was going to be a doctor.

Twelve

BACULUS: a most valuable word. It is Latin for rod. In it lies the origins of the word *bacillus* (and also, via a Greek etymological cousin, *bacterium*). The Latin word *imbecillus* means 'without a stick', as in 'walking stick', and mutated somewhat in its journey through the French – *pace* Pip Chumley – it gives us the word imbecile. But it is through the word *débacle* that *baculus* really achieves true glory, for it means 'stick-removal', as in unbarring a door, or perhaps, more expressively, removing a stick from a dam.

That's what happened upon returning to Ratcliffe the following autumn. Heretofore I had been gambolling in an academic paddling pool. Now I was suddenly drowning in a cataract. In part it was the subjects themselves. However, it wasn't just their numbing difficulty, but my sheer grief-stricken inability to remember anything remotely valuable. There was a third force: I had been finally hit by a dam burst of teenage testosterone. That summer and autumn, aged sixteen and a half, my voice had finally broken, and the flood waters of neo-manhood, with all its idiocies, infirmities and delinquent appetites, had washed through my helpless body.

Different emotions and hormones were suddenly warring with me for regional dominance. I cackled, I sulked, I brooded,

I laughed, I frowned, I grew angry, and most of all, I was baffled by the simplest things. It was as if my cerebral-emotional control board had been randomly rewired, with a diabolical master-circuit ensuring that no response to any particular phenomenon was ever appropriate. Most of all, academically, I was a true debacle. Nothing registered in my imbecilic brain.

AND THEN of course there was sex. Libido took command of my body. Lust inhabited my brain and groin and my heart, a priapic compulsion of quite magnetic and maddening power. But I was still a Catholic. I truly believed in all the rules of the Church, even if now I didn't manage to go to Mass every day. It was Church doctrine that sexual impurity was a mortal sin. I had had four years of living with this house-devil, 'mortal sin', roaming my mental attic, so I simply wasn't going to take a return trip into the horrors of mortal-sin land. Lust therefore remained unsated. I would not even touch myself, ever, no matter how grave the temptation. Each morning I awoke with an erection and I dressed with an erection and went to breakfast with an erection, pulsing vehicles of ardent lust that yearned to be touched, and of its own accord, eagerly sought the friction against my trousers for release of some kind. But I wouldn't allow my very personal enemy and live-in foe even the slightest release. I tolerated absolutely nothing that might be sensual or sinful. I was a slave to anti-pleasure.

What probably made this virtue all the more excruciating was that I never had any wet dreams. Like a miser with his gold in a garret, my scrotum retained all its reproductive fluids, and its many trillions of seeds. At times I became almost demented with lust, and got headaches and backaches and stomach aches. I couldn't think of anything else, while that autonomous being at the other end of my young Catholic body remained in permanent and tumescent uproar. Whenever I tried to study, the Satanic republic between my legs start an uprising that would require all my concentration to control: yearning, not learning, was the sole result of study.

As a sixth-former I now shared a room with a boy named Iain Baker, who one night after lights out, whispered to me that he was in bad trouble: he couldn't stop masturbating. 'But you've got to stop,' I replied through the dark. 'It's a mortal sin.'

'I know, I know. But I can't. I just can't. Once you've started, you can't stop.'

'That's why I'm never going to start,' I swore. For I actually wanted to prove to Iain it was possible to be 'pure'. I was a Catholic who still sought to do the right thing, and to set an example for Iain. Yes, I still believed.

Generally, I was overwhelmed with confusion and ignorance about myself and my body, and so it seemed all part of the same boundless delirium that as we walked into supper, one of the Gallagher brothers turned to me and said, 'Kennedy's been shot.'

Kennedy was the English teacher, a wiry man from Newcastle with a thick Geordie accent, so I assumed that there must have been an accident on the school shooting range.

'Mr Kennedy? But he's even not in the CCF.'

'No, not him. President Kennedy.'

Someone had shot the hero of our times? Quite impossible. Another mad notion to barge its way into my brain and take up valuable space. Yet even as I was putting the absurd idea aside, I found the refectory all abuzz as the word whirred round at impossible speed, like an atom particle in a cyclotron. Beetle Moss walked in, his face as grey as an old headstone. He spoke to Father Nann at the head table, and then went back past my table towards the door.

'How is he, Father?' inquired John Stanley.

'Dead,' he whispered, and 300 boys convulsed like a frog's leg on Galvani's electric lathe. Only in later years did we learn of the true rottenness that was at the heart of the Kennedy cult. But back then, it seemed as if an entire civilization was going; had we not long before just lost Pope John XXIII? And more personally, one by one, the shutters had been falling on the old world of my life. Mr Thom, Dad, Uncle Harry, the Pope and President Kennedy had all passed in that single year. Two weeks after the killing in Dallas, Michael Parker – yes, that jolly, awkward, frightfully frightfully decent gentleman – was stabbed through the heart in his surgery by a deranged patient. His terrible dying screams alerted Nonie, who ran in to find the happy killer holding the carving knife, beaming, and covered in blood. He sat down and politely asked her to call the police.

The world might have been rocking and adolescence had robbed me of most of my faculties, but I could be in no doubt about the academic debacle that was befalling me. One evening I saw, with shocking clarity, what was happening to my life. I knew I must act. I went to Jack Morris, to ask permission to change courses. He looked at me wordlessly while I faltered through my explanation, his dark eyes staring over the pale steeple of his cadaverous fingers. I hurriedly assured him that I'd work extra hours to catch up if I were only allowed to study English, French and history.

He paused for a while. 'I have to tell you, Myers,' he replied finally, 'that I am highly dissatisfied with both your work and your conduct. If it weren't for your mother, I would ask you to leave the school. So listen here, young fellow. You'll just have to buck up, or by golly, I'll jolly well send you packing.'

'But I know things aren't going well, sir. That's why I want to change to do arts subjects.'

'Do you think we're here to attend to your every whim? You've made your choice, now be a man and stick with it. You've taken up enough of my time already. Good night.'

I returned to the calamity that was my academic life and worked extra hard on being pleasant to the unfortunate creatures who were supervising my descent into academic perdition.

IT'S POINTLESS even trying to describe the hell of that first Christmas without Dad. Mum was in dire straits financially, reduced to giving board and bed to strangers. Poor Maggy was going out to work every Saturday to earn a few extra shillings. Johnny's childhood lay in ruins. David was working in a school in New Zealand, unable to contact anyone, nursing his grief alone. Bill was trying to make ends meet in Oxford, and Ann, Michael and their daughter Katy-Ann were living in one room with Mum while Michael looked for a job. Every back was bearing an intolerable and endless burden. I saw no escape. I toyed with the idea of running away and joining the Irish Guards, but that was sheer fantasy, for it would break Mum's heart. Anyway, I'd be as useless at that as I was at my studies. Indeed, I was uniquely incompetent at everything, apart from rugby and hockey, but not quite alone in misery – merely ignorant of the fullness of what others were enduring.

The second sixth-form term confirmed my worst fears. No matter how hard I worked, no matter how many hours I put in, I remembered nothing of the new disciplines of biology, physics and chemistry. I took to rising before dawn, and, making a tent with a towel over my desk lamp so as not to wake Iain, I would study before the rest of the school rose. But to no avail. I would find that I was merely extending the hours of almost unbearable sexual temptation, and learning nothing.

I took to seeing more of Richard Burgess, who was now sharing a room with Andrew Campbell. He was a handsome, gifted boy, almost uniquely cultured in this most philistine of islands. He still threw clay, and could happily discuss art and music. I started visiting him when I knew Andrew was elsewhere. We talked about The Beatles and Benjamin Britten, sex and girls. He too asked me if I ever masturbated. I told him no, adding randomly, 'Anyway, I think it's mostly queers who do that.'

'I'm not queer, but I do it.'

'But it's a mortal sin, isn't it?'

'My sister told me it isn't.'

'Your sister?'

'Yes, she told me she does it, and it's natural.'

'Your sister *really* told you that?'

'Oh yes. We're very open in our family. She even told me when she lost her virginity. She told Mummy too. Mummy said that was good, because she really should have sex with a few men before she got married – that's what she did.'

Clearly, it seemed that the Burgesses were exempt from the rules that commanded my life. But the teenage brain moves in weird loops, impossible to divine, for I remember that Richard then complained about his complexion. His nose was regularly beset with blackheads, and he next described in lurid detail what had popped out when he squeezed them, while I listened in awed fascination. I realized I truly adored him.

One Friday evening Iain came back from the weekly confession with astounding news. Father Elson had told him to stop worrying about masturbation. It wasn't such a grievous sin, and it certainly wasn't a mortal sin.

I was quiet for a while. 'Are you sure?'

'Absolutely sure. He just said that one should try to show personal self discipline.'

Well, that sounded just like the sort of moral order I could understand. That night I waited until the entire school slept, and around midnight, I finally decided to rid myself of the torment of lust that had nearly driven me mad. The only sound came from above, as the lanyard slapped against the flagpole on the old bell tower from which I had once seen Saturn. My heart was racing like hooves down the final furlong as I pulled back the blankets, and to the steady rhythm of the flagpole's meditations, I finally and joyfully surrendered to lust. However, as I was soon to discover, satisfying teenage lust is really like foreign devils trying to rule China: even an amiable and just governance never quite precludes the possibility of a sudden and bloody insurrection. Lust slaked does not mean lust slain.

Nor was the need for sex satisfied by my own efforts. Richard remained in the forefront of my mind. Several times in his room, I came close to kissing him, but the taboos on this were too powerful. It's not that my desires seemed perverse – quite the opposite; they seemed right – but I also knew they were somehow unacceptable. It didn't make sense, but of course, nothing did.

The prefects for the next year were announced at term's end. They included Stuart Morecambe, who was staying on for a place at Oxbridge, as head prefect, with Conan Kavanagh as his deputy. John Stanley, Dave Ploughman and John O'Malley were all appointed prefects, but I wasn't. I was grievously disappointed, though of course this was not a logical response. What offended me most of all was that an amiable Boer called Freddie Van Huitzenberg, a year below me, was appointed prefect. To be bested by a Catholic Afrikaaner, a species I never previously knew existed, was a rare distinction indeed.

That summer I got a job in Lewis's department store in the centre of Leicester. It was five storeys over basement, a little Harrods of the Midlands. I worked six days a week for £5 a week. Every penny I earned, for the first three weeks, after tax and insurance, went in repaying Richard Taylor for his radio. That was the price for my impulsive prudishness. The final week's income went to Mum.

Upon my return to Ratcliffe, Morris called me to his office. A prefect's vacancy had arisen. What he was proposing was, he said, more to honour my brothers' achievements rather to reward any promise I had shown. But would I be a prefect? Now, being a prefect brought some privileges. One could wear a dark suit or a sports jacket instead of the school uniform. And I desperately craved status, which a different attire would surely help me achieve, as too might an officially bestowed authority. I instantly said yes.

The following Saturday I went in to Leicester to buy clothes that would befit my new elevated status. However, aware of how desperately straitened was our economic position, I knew I had to buy as cheaply as possible. The very first sports jacket that I tried on was a sensational bargain, as the nice salesman at John Colliers, 'Gentlemen's Clothiers', freely admitted. It was made of brand-new man-made fibres that were completely free of that nasty old-fashioned wool.

'Sir, being young, I'm sure appreciates the need to keep clothing à la mode. Had sir been here yesterday, he might have got one of the herringbone pattern. But no matter! This one – a tasteful autumn russet, very fetching – is just as fine. And might I suggest some of these rather elegant nylon shirts to go with it? The bargain of the season, two for the price of three. Sir is also looking for a suit? Allow me to introduce sir to an entirely new concept in menswear, a two-piece suit made entirely of plastic derivatives. A better bargain – if I may be so bold – even than the jacket and them there tasteful shirts. The last of a line that we're now discontinuing, mistakenly, in my opinion, but oh boy, if I may be so bold, is sir in luck 'ere, with a 40 per cent discount!'

I disappeared into the changing-room, and when I emerged, the salesman nearly shied in ecstasy.

'Ah,' he whinnied. 'Just look at the cut of them trousers!'

His hand reached out and seized hold of a large fold of fabric just above my bottom, and together we gazed admiringly into the mirror, his arm behind me like a ventriloquist with his dummy.

'The waist's still a little wide for sir just yet, but sir is growing. A good belt will do the trick: though I say it myself, quite the bargain of the season!'

I didn't hesitate and bought the suit, sports jacket and the tasteful shirts and triumphantly sailed back to school. And only over the coming days did I realize how truly gruesome the sports jacket was. It was an essay in chemicals ending in '–ene', all of which had apparently been glued together, so giving it a strange metallic sheen, and accompanied by the almost-permanent crackle of static electricity. When worn with the nylon shirts, it turned into a miniature power-station, and in the dark, I actually sparkled, a walking *son et lumière* enactment of adolescent hopelessness.

The suit, meanwhile, possessed a feature that had escaped my earlier attention. Not merely was the waist too wide, the bottom was absolutely massive: room enough two. But *nil desperandum*! I was a boy scout, so that night I stitched an inward fold into the seat, reckoning that, provided I wasn't too energetic, the improvised seam, aided by a sturdy belt, would surely hold together. Thus attired, I ventured forth from my own little room, for my very first breakfast as a suited prefect.

'What's that you've got on?' hissed Richard Burgess as I entered the refectory.

'My new suit.'

'New?' he cried. 'It's an Italian bloody teddy-boy outfit.'

He was right. In my frenzy to get the bargain of a lifetime, I had actually managed to buy the sartorial equivalent of Dad's Mark II Ford Zodiac. The jacket was cut in an almost bolero style, without the mandatory flap in the rear. For boys of taste and distinction, not having the flap was socially like not having trousers. But far worse was its length – the bottom of the jacket barely reached halfway down my buttocks.

Once again, desperate situations require desperate remedies. Gazing at myself in the mirror, I found that if I pressed my shoulders backwards and downwards, the manoeuvre could lower the very bottom of the jacket that little bit extra. This also required for me to stick my stomach out. I thus became the pioneer of an entirely new gait, combining a forward assertion of the abdomen with a backward inclination of the shoulders. However, one further adjustment was required to perfect the image of Kevin Myers, boulevardier. The onrush of hormones had, I felt, caused my nose to grow far too much. Moreover, it had a rounded tip, just like my father's – and tragically unlike the neat and aquiline adornment on my mother's face, which she had thoughtfully passed on to every single member of my family except for me. So, after careful practice before the mirror, I concluded that by using my facial muscles to hold my nose downwards in a sort of semi-permanent moue, I might in time make the result – a slightly diminished bulb – a permanent feature of my face. By willpower alone, I was going to defeat the destiny ordained for me by DNA, and reshape the contours of my face.

So enter the newest prefect in the corridors of Ratcliffe College! Observe him, cruising along the corridors in his cockerel strut, with his shoulders arched back and his belly forward, a scintillating mass of noisy sparks, a crackling, one-man Aurora Borealis, the kind of passenger that is so sizzling and irresistible that he would have been statute-barred from travelling on a Zeppelin. See his lower face, almost permanently contorted by his heroic efforts to cultivate an aquiline nose by willpower alone. In other words, see sad Malvolio, in his crossed garters and yellow stockings!

Meanwhile, Dave Ploughman stunned us all with the revelation that he was the first to lose his virginity. He had been on holiday in Dublin with his father, and had met a girl on Portmarnock golf links, who had arranged to see him after the game. She had promptly deflowered Dave behind a dune. It was, he said, the most amazingly beautiful thing of all time. What? Loose women in Ireland? That didn't seem possible: not in the land of my saintly aunts with portly bottoms.

My mind was also on sex, but increasingly via the person of cool, laconic Richard Burgess. He, being elegantly indifferent to the narcotic of power, had not been made a prefect, so we now moved in different circles. But this did not abate my still-deranged interest in him, and I hungered to be with him in some undetermined intimate way, for my desire remained utterly incoherent. What would any 'intimacy' actually involve? Yes, of course, sex of some kind. But whereas masturbation by oneself might not now be a grave matter, with another boy, it might be a return to the deadly land of mortal sin. How on earth could I find out? At this stage in world history, it still wasn't possible to ask a priest: 'Excuse me Father, is it okay for me to wank another boy off? But don't worry, I think I'm in love with him.'

There was also the practical side. Where could one safely do anything? And what if one were caught? The answer to the second question was simple: ignominious and calamitous expulsion. And that was it, the worst fate that could befall any boy at Ratcliffe, and something that most boys had discussed, and agreed: nothing compared with the sheer public shame of expulsion. There was even a salutary tale within Ratcliffe's folklore of the boy who was expelled and managed to keep the news from his mother with his father's approval. His father secretly collected him from school, and as they approached the gates of the driveway onto the main road, the distressed father drove into the pillar and broke his ribcage on the steering wheel, killing himself instantly. The boy was found hours later, paralyzed with shock. The real potency of this no doubt fictional myth was that he then had to break the bad news of his explusion to his mother.

For it was maternal disapproval, and worse, maternal disappointment, which were the binary nightmares of all the boys. Because, firstly, it was quite clear that all mothers were complete strangers to lust, so they couldn't possibly understand what might have driven their sons to sexual mischief; and whatever else we boys thought and did, our mothers – and their love – were truly holy, sacrosanct and inviolate.

In rugby, I was playing for the school's First XV, which of course, proved to be the very worst in the entire history of the school: by season's end, we had played eleven, lost eleven. One ritual did not vanish with defeat. John O'Malley had got into the habit, whenever the scrum collapsed, of shouting 'Ooo me balls,' most especially if young females were nearby. Then he would be the last to rise, and after looking ruefully at the girls, would trot after his disappearing forwards. It was an unusual way of winning female hearts, and prompted his nickname Tender Testes.

The high point of Ratcliffe's year was the Feast of Immaculate Conception, generally known as the Immac. I knew that the prefects would have to sing the school song at the end of the banquet, which, I was sure, no one knew. So I got Peedum to produce Gestetnered copies of it, and arranged for another boy to collect them while I played rugby against the Old Boys – who, as it turned out, largely consisted of cripples left over from the Normandy landings. It made no difference – we lost, thanks to a last-minute penalty, accidentally but typically conceded by me.

That night came the much-anticipated banquet. For the older boys, a glass of wine was served with dinner, and a generous allowance of port followed. However, two of the prefects had earlier sneaked in and managed to purloin some extra of bottles of port, which they hid under the table, and were being consumed freely. As always, some venerable Old Ratcliffians, rubicund survivors of the Crimea, had stayed to dine and to favour us with speeches that were their imitations of Frettie Fox's sermons, while the prefects' table descended into inebriate anarchy.

Then it was time for us to sing the ancient school song, 'Floreat Ratcliffia'. But the Gestetnered copies of the words had been mislaid by the relevant prefect, who'd got at the port long before dinner, so we all rose without the words. We knew the first line; the rest was a trifle vague, even for those of us who were sober. So, having unshipped the opening phrase or two, we launched into an improvised medley of words and a bawled refrain, 'Ratcliffe, BLAH BLAH BLAH endless generations praise BLAH BLAH Ratcliffe ways, Floreat floreat floreat Ratcliffia!'

The chorus was meant to be sung by the entire school and the assembled swells of Old Ratcliffians, but we had thoroughly baffled them with our attempts at a first verse, and where there should have been the swelling roar of several hundred boys and the stout veterans of El Alamein, there was just the pub babble of drunken prefects.

We attacked the second verse, but since we did so without even the benefit of a first line, from the outset it consisted of, atonally: 'TUMPTY TUMPTY TUM, BLAH-DE BLAH DE BLAH.' Finally, the president of the Old Ratcliffians' Society rang the refectory bell and with a face as dark as a thundercloud rose to address the school. 'Enough,' he boomed, as a handful of prefects wept hysterically. 'You have brought dishonour to the old school with that pitiful farrago. You should be ashamed! Ashamed, I say, ashamed! Silence, if you please.'

He sat down, glaring with roseate wrath, and the prefects of Ratcliffe College slid into a still deeper dissolution.

One night while I was on dormitory duty, a rather pretty French boy (well he was) named Montmorency asked me if there was something especially *British* about the Immac's proceedings, because whatever it was, he couldn't understand it. Montmorency was at Ratcliffe because during the war, his father had come to revere British ways and British decency. That drunken ineptitude, amongst the most untalented generation in the school's history, might be the simple explanation. He looked at me with wistfully innocent eyes. Unable to concoct a lie, I told him all would become clear in time. As indeed it did.

Meanwhile, I proceeded with an adolescence that seemed composed of failure, lust and ineptitude while about my prefectorial duties I possessed the natural authority of Stan Laurel, though perhaps not always possessing his sartorial élan. I was tolerated by my peers, largely because I didn't lack physical courage, but I was a figure of fun to the younger boys. This I could have borne with resignation, but for the fact that my young brother Johnny was now in First Year, and was witness to my daily humiliations. I was least unhappy alone in my room. Like the other boys, I made coffee simply by directly pouring water from the hot water tap onto instant Nescafé and adding Fussell's tinned milk. We would speculate on how many rats a year were boiled alive in the hot water system, but we still drank the water. The obligatory daytime snack for all boys was Ritz Crackers, of which, because I could afford just two packets a term, I would have one per day.

My mid-morning coffee one day not merely tasted terrible, but had a strangely glutinous quality to it. I threw it away. Two evenings later, sitting at my desk in my room, I felt ill with desire for Richard, his body, his affections, his imaginary kisses. I knew that this was Andrew Campbell's bath night, and Richard would be in their room alone. So just before lights out, I capitulated. Shoelessly I left my room and stole across the school to the far wing. Every silent yard of the journey was fraught with peril. Regardless of spiritual consequence, I intended to do unholy things to Richard's body. One thing was blessedly certain: he of all people would have no qualms about sex. How could he, since both his sister and mother were clearly nymphomaniacs?

Richard was reading in bed when I arrived. I whispered to him to put on his dressing-gown and follow me. Almost as if waiting for this moment, he obediently did so, and together we glided through those long dark silent corridors like ghosts' shadows, to the accompanying artillery salvoes of my heart, and the merry electric crackle of my clothes. Finally, I got him to my room, closed the door behind him, and without more ado I reached into his dressing-gown.

'Stop!' he said, staying my hand. 'I've something to tell you.'

Puzzled, I plopped down on my bed. Inwardly, I was like a gundog panting on its leash. Richard sat in the small wooden chair behind my desk, but facing me. I could see his erection under his pyjamas. 'I know what you want. I want it too,' he whispered thickly. 'I came here the other night. I wanted to wake you and kiss you and make you come.'

'What do you mean, you came here?'

'I came in here. About one in the morning. I was standing right beside your bed. While you slept. I was going to wake you, but then I lost my nerve. I thought you might say no. But I was so absolutely fucking demented. I've felt anything so bad like it in my life. I had to do something about it. So I had a wank into your basin.'

'Not my basin,' I intoned hollowly. 'My fucking coffee cup.'

But I was elated. I knew what this meant. I reached out, and again he pushed my hand aside.

'We can't. Not now we can't.'

'Why not? You wanted to the other night, didn't you?'

'Yes I did, and I do now ... look.' He gestured downwards. Had he taken his cock out, he would never have left that room alive.

'For fuck's sake, Richard!'

'Listen!' he said. 'You don't understand.'

And as lights went off across the school, and the final liquid silence of the night fell everywhere else, he told me two stories. The first tale concerned the time he fell ill during a school epidemic when he was fifteen and the school infirmary was full, so he was confined to his dormitory, alone. One afternoon, a Rosminian named Brother Hickey arrived and offered to massage his belly. After a while, Hickey had complained that the pyjama cord was getting in the way, and so he opened it. His hand went lower, and then began to caress Richard's penis. The brother had then masturbated him.

'It was sort of nice but really horrible at the same time. I knew it was wrong. So did Brother Hickey. The moment I'd come, he apologized, and went away, and came back a few minutes later with Father Hastings. Father Hastings told me that what we'd both done was sinful, and he had better hear my confession. So I made my confession to him, and he said all would be well, provided I didn't tell anyone.'

'But that's nothing to do with us,' I howled.

'Yes it is. Last year Brother O'Dwyer got me in his room. He did it to me, just like Hickey. I felt terrible afterwards. So I told Father Hastings, and he said that it must have been my fault. I was clearly an occasion of sin, and that unless I was very careful, I could go to hell.'

'But you came in my coffee cup last week!' I protested.

'Yes, and afterwards I knew that was wrong, so I went and told Father Hastings, and he congratulated me, and said that I had shown that I could triumph over my wicked nature, and I must always do so again.'

In despair and disbelief, I said, 'So why did you come here tonight?'

'To tell you that I think I'm in love with you.'

I reached out and touched his knee, and he put his hand on mine. I was quite ill with desire and emotion and all the confused heart-and-loin bedlam of a teenager. Then I tried to push my hand up his thigh. He pushed it back.

'Can't we even feel one another?' I asked plaintively.

'No. Hastings said a sin that is committed in specific violation of an undertaking given to a priest really is a mortal sin.'

'Are we never going to do it?' I asked incredulously.

'I don't see how we can.'

We talked for hours about our feelings for one another. We admitted that we each longed to kiss and caress one another's bodies, and to make one another come. My poor teen manhood throbbed with lust and disappointment. Richard left long after midnight, and my solitary heart passed unseen through the long corridors with him. But I lived in hope. There must surely be another night.

Thirteen

THAT CHRISTMAS term, the family moved out of 17 Medina Road, while I was still at school. Neighbours dropped in notes regretting our departure; one was from the Eddicks – for, despite the Myers' erroneous aspirations of their name, it had no 'h' in it after all. So I went 'home' to the new Myers house at New Way Road in Evington on the far side of the city. There was no farewell from me to Medina Road, as there had been no farewell to Dad.

On my return to Ratcliffe for the spring term, I'd hoped to become goalkeeper for the First XI hockey team, but Conan Kavanagh had stayed on, and so I remained in the Second XI. That was to prove an important separation, for that hockey First XI became the core of a fresh and subversive élite in the school. At its head was the skipper and head prefect, Stuart Morecambe. He was a likeable, commanding figure, but he was quite unlike any of the head boys of previous years. Firstly, he didn't even try to seem like a gentleman, and in this lack of affectation he was showing the only honest aspect of his personality, for at bottom he was a scheming and endlessly artful spiv.

Smoking cigarettes was regarded as a very serious offence in Ratcliffe, for which boys could actually be expelled, whereas prefects, in recognition of their godlike status, were allowed to smoke pipes. So each evening, half a dozen teenagers would sit in the prefects' common room, gravely puffing on pipes, like RAF squadron commanders waiting for the message to scramble, chaps. However, not merely was Stuart Morecambe a secret cigarette smoker, but he was the school's primary dealer in the weed. Indeed, he traded in a wide range of merchandise, including girlie mags and booze, sold with the assistance of half a dozen prefects, whose clientele thus gained immunity from all all other school rules.

Most spectacularly, Stuart's enterprise proved so profitable that his gang was able to buy a car, which they hid in old farm buildings, and in which they'd go off on pub jaunts after lights out. Their indiscreet antics proved how powerful was the schoolboy culture of omertà, for no one squealed. As it happened, Stuart's lieutenants, John O'Malley, Conan Kavanagh, John Stanley and Dave Ploughman, were in their own way decent lads. I certainly didn't disapprove of what they were doing, though I was a unsure of the appropriateness of prefects simultaneously running both the rule of law and the main opposition to it.

As the only prefect who also a senior scout, I was now in charge of the school firefighting team; a pleasing familial coincidence. We had a petrol-driven hand-pushed pump, and each Wednesday afternoon, while most of my peers sullenly trooped off to the martial tedium of cadet parades, I led Ratcliffe's boy scout fire brigade in putting out imaginary infernos in different parts of the school. I discovered that one length of hose was shorter than all the others, and if attached to the out pipe from the pump could lead to what might be a disastrous lack of length. So I had its brass fittings marked with white paint, and insisted that all the boys be aware that it was only to be used as a source connecting the mains with the pump, and never as a fire hose.

Meanwhile, chemistry and physics lessons had moved on to almost Hebraic realms of incomprehensibility. I knew that I was sailing towards the rocks of an academic Cape of No Hope, but nonetheless felt that hope of some kind lay in biology. Until the day, that is, that some smiling green frogs were brought into the lab in a glass tank. That kindly old assassin, Primavesi, cackled as he filled their home with chloroform, and a few minutes later, their limp damp corpses were distributed for dissection.

I utterly detested the gratuitous murder of these affable little fellows. How I loathed having to explore their intimate innards. It didn't matter that the frogs didn't suffer, or that their guts are almost colour-coded, which made the task of dissection relatively easy for those who considered that teasing out a stranger's pancreas with tempered steel was a proper way to spend an adolescence.

Rabbits were even worse. Their day also began and ended with Primavesi wielding the chloroform. After a minute's silence each of us was given a cadaver, which we pinned onto our personal dissecting board, like a furry baby. First a slice, from sternum to groin; and oh the stench, as a warm, vanilla-like fragrance closed over one's face. It was like wearing a gas mask made of entrails. I toiled with a baffled blade through these innards, a freshly dreadful stink with each new incision. No doubt it was right for future medical students to be doing this, but not me: for I knew that for once and for all, I had passed from their ranks, as I toiled at nature's workbench of warm liver and slithery lights, gagging repeatedly.

Primavesi was no prude. He enthusiastically directed us all over the rabbit, and naturally we went sleuthing towards the genitals, even though they were remarkably uninspiring. The penis was a tiny nub, like a small mole in its groin. However, Prim cautioned, with sexual arousal, one would probably find that the penis was considerably perkier than the sad little specimens we were now examining. 'But,' he chortled merrily, 'ewection is unlikely to occur in the pwesent circumstances, tee hee hee.'

One boy, Brian Byrne, was dissecting a doe, unsuccessfully foraging through her lady parts until, maddened with frustration, he no doubt spoke for generations of men about similarly futile quests when he wailed despairingly, 'Please sir, I can't find her clitoris.'

Spring was here, and the bees in Primavesi's hives attached to the laboratory windows began to bestir themselves beyond their glass viewing panels. The entire biology wing began to reek of nectar and honey, but the gazing Primavesi only scowled at his teeming little pets. 'Wuffians!' he cursed through the pane as the she-workers returned from their explorations, laden with pollen and the sweetness of the fields. 'Wuffians! I can smell that tweacherous weed, the dandelion! Turning my pwecious hive into a uwinal!'

Prim was an odd man, a living relic of those ancients that had brought the honeybee from southern Europe to these Atlantic shores some 1500 years ago. He was single-minded and tough, but kindly too, in an austere, emotionless way. I was looking at his bees with him that final spring of my schooldays, and without turning to me he murmured, 'You're not really cut out for all this, my boy. You do know that, don't you?'

'Yes sir,' I said, and together in silence the two of us continued gazing at his bees. A third presence silently joined us at that glass screen, and it went by the name of Failure.

IN THE common room, the boys listened to Beatles music and smoked pipes and talked about girls. Dave Ploughman had borrowed his father's collection of big band music, to which I became a convert. I loved the drumming of Gene Krupa, Buddy Rich and Louis Bellson. Despite my poverty, I had somehow managed to buy an album by The Clancy Brothers and Tommy Makem, which served as a real emotional link to Ireland. 'The Rocky Road to Dublin' had a rhythmical structure that was as complex and stirring and as Irish as the big bands were American, and 'The West's Awake' was to my mind everything that an Irish song should be, with a haunting melody and a triumphant and patriotic conclusion. Two Murphy cousins, Hugh and Bernard, a couple of years younger than me and from a fabulously rich family of scrap-dealers, were part of my secret Irish music freemasonry. More than that, they were advertisements for my idealized Irishness, being both intellectually and athletically brilliant.

Allow me to reintroduce Dawson, the fine fellow who in my second year would rise each morning sporting a visible erection, like a mizzenmast butting its way around the horniest of Horns. He was now the mainstay of the swimming team, which that June had its annual family-day gala. The swimmers emerged in a line and removed their tracksuits, revealing that Dawson had brought his erection with him, with which he proceeded to nonplus the parents as he sauntered around the pool.

In due course, Dawson rose and stood on his starting block, flexing his legs and smirking, his penis throbbing like a muzzled camel tongue. His mother, sitting in the front seat, was peering this way and that, with a bizarre proprietorial pride, while everyone else was silently urging the starter to fire his fucking gun. An eternity elapsed before he did so, and it was neither Dawson's feet nor his hands that first broke the surface of the water. Predictably, perhaps aided by his keel, he won, and predictably, he was awarded the cup, which he raised over his head, while his manhood performed similarly in front of him.

Only members of the swimming club were allowed in the pool afterwards. Gazing at them cavorting through cool water on a hot summer's day, Richard scowled: 'This isn't fucking fair. What about us having a midnight skinny dip?' I instantly and lasciviously assented. He said he'd wake me in my room. That night I had barely fallen asleep when I felt Richard's hand on my shoulder. I instantly rose, put on my dressing-gown, grabbed a towel and giddily followed him down the dark corridors to the exit. He unbolted the back door, and we walked out through the night to the pool. We slipped out of our dressing-gowns and pyjamas. The hot day had been replaced by a bitterly icy night.

I rested a toe on the water. It was as cold and hard as a midwinter boilerplate. I slowly lowered myself in. Each inch of water felt like a vice agonizingly closing over my legs until the terrible centre of gravity was reached, and cold teeth closed on my testicles, which withdrew instantly to the canals from which they had fled eighteen years earlier.

I swam away from the side, gasping frantically. It was like swimming in an arctic version of napalm. I even felt my liver go cold while I doggy-paddled with a quiet frenzy, both to stay alive and to stay afloat. Richard slipped in, and was instantly keening with pain. In the pale glow of stars and moon, I saw his head bobbing in the water like a seal's. Yet though I was physically incapable of desire, my heart and mind and lips remained true to a heroically remembered carnal duty: I must have him.

I swam towards him, while the flesh on my fingers first puckered and then withered away completely. But I did not care. I would reach out with those frozen corpse's hands and caress his body and kiss his lips. And then, as I came closer to him, I heard footsteps approaching from the school. Oh Christ almighty. We were about to be found out. Desire died. I instantly breaststroked over to Richard.

'We're in trouble,' I whispered, through lifeless, ice-cold lips. 'Someone's coming.'

'It's all right. It's probably Martin.'

'Martin? What the fuck … ?'

'I'll tell you later.'

'Hiya chaps,' bellowed a voice, as if this were early afternoon in St Tropez.

'Shhhh,' we both hissed.

Martin slipped out of his nightclothes and splashed into the water like a walrus.

'Christ, it's flipping freezing,' he yodelled heartily upward to the coldly blinking stars. After a few minutes of following one another in futile, icebound circles, the three of us got out of the pool and towelled ourselves down. Our teeth chattered like the disconnected keys of a piano being pushed downstairs.

'Shall we go for a stroll?' I suggested, hoping that Martin would choose go back to bed. I might as well have hoped for a geyser to douse us with warm water. We walked up beyond the Second XI cricket pitch to the old airfield. I said: 'I'm going for a run. Anyone coming?'

I was hoping Richard would follow, so that we could vanish into the night and do terrible, unspeakable, glorious things to one another's bodies. I stepped out of my nightwear, and barefoot, loped nakedly away, silently urging Richard to follow, He did not. So I ran alone into the vast moonless dark around the field, over which an old Ratcliffian barely older than I was now had once circled futilely. After an equally futile circuit, though at a more modest altitude, I rejoined the others, and we all chastely returned our rooms.

I didn't see Richard again until the following evening.

'Why did you tell that idiot Martin about the swim?'

'I just let it slip out. And he asked if he could join us. I could hardly say no.'

'Then let's go tonight, just the two of us!'

'No we can't. I saw Father Hastings this morning and told him about last night. He said Martin's presence was the grace of God preventing us from committing mortal sin. We were lucky, he says.'

'Lucky?' I cried.

'Lucky. We can't do it, ever, don't you see?'

IN A LAST vain attempt to put my academic life to rights, I embarked upon a frenzy of study. I would stay up late and get up early. Each dawn, I heard the old milk train rattling along the tracks as it stopped at the farmers' halts between Nottingham and Leicester, and as it reached Sileby station, it would blow its steam whistle. Then the distant clatter of steel on steel would fade, and I would return to the yawning emptiness of my mind, the Sanskrit of my textbooks and the torment of my lust.

One Monday in the general Sixth-Form common room Richard and I were listening to Ravel on the BBC Third Programme. The bell went for study time in our rooms. Richard turned to me and said: 'Look … I keep thinking about having sex with you, and it's driving me crazy. I'll come to your room in ten minutes. But what if anyone sees me?' Visits to other boys' rooms during study time were forbidden. I handed him my fountain pen.

'Tell them that you're returning this.'

I went to my room and waited, my stomach foul with nausea and heaving with yearning. Finally, the door opened very quietly, and Richard stole in, his face glowing with decision and desire. I rose from my desk, and reached out for him. The moment had finally arrived. As we were about to kiss, metal-heeled footsteps came clicking down the corridor and we spiralled apart. The door opened. It was Robbo, a dour Scottish physics teacher.

'Burgess! I thought so – I just saw you entering the block. What are you doing here doing study hour?'

'I just came to return this pen, sir.' It was already in his hand.

'Very well. Now off you go.'

As Richard left my room, our eyes met. I sensed that a last chance had just been seized from me. Yet I yearned to impress him, and shortly afterwards, we were to have the final Open Day of the year, when parents and family would visit the school. He told me his parents were bringing his sister Valerie – would I like to meet her? Well, considering what I had learned about her, most certainly!

Open Day duly arrived, and I was much excited, because the fire brigade were to down as the star turn. A smoke canister was to be ignited in an upstairs window and my fire team would douse the inferno and save the school from disaster. Richard came round to the scout hut shortly before the performance began, and with him was Valerie. She was twenty, like a very female Richard, and her loveliness was made even more bewitching by my knowledge that she regularly had orgasms alone.

'You're going to put out the fire, Richard tells me. You fire-fighting types must be very brave.'

'Not brave,' I replied with a manly nonchalance. 'Merely doing our duty.'

My heart was thumping with joyous lust: brother and sister – I wasn't sure which one I fancied the more.

'I'm really looking forward to the display,' she sighed. 'There's something very sexy about firemen. The hose … so very phallic. I wish I could hold it with you.'

She smiled me with winning eyes. Yes, yes, she could be mine!

The pair of them left, and my team assembled. Soon afterwards, the siren went, and Ratcliffe College's fire brigade swung into action. We jog-trotted the pump round the side of the assembly hall, across the cricket pitch, right to the front of the school, around which several hundred parents were gathered in a wide arc. Like clockwork, my team dispersed about their tasks as the pump was connected to the mains and I connected the front hose to its intermediary lengths. Myself and two other boys raced to the tower, but only then discovered that we had inadvertently incorporated the short length to the firehose, instead of using it to connect the pump to the mains. I was thus at least twenty feet short of the building when we ran out of hose.

'Pump on!' I bellowed with a querulous authority.

The pump roared into life, and we braced ourselves for the kick as the surging torrent arrived at the business end of the hose. A surging torrent it might have been, but it was not strong enough to make up the shortage of hose length. Instead of the water pouring into the open window, it fell in rainbow cascades on the flowerbed in front of the building. I stood there, trying to look heroic, while the rest of my crew tactfully melted into the crowd, which was itself dispersing amid a general air of acute embarrassment. And of Valerie, there was no sign, then or ever again.

A larger calamity was awaiting me: my A Levels. And I was right, for they became an extended valley of death that in its sheer awfulness stands quite alone in my life. I have no real memory of the papers, just a general sense of a catastrophe, day after day. Wars have come and gone in my life, men have died beside me, and I have loved and lost more than I decently should. But the one great abiding nightmare that returns to haunt my sleep is of repeatedly sitting down to exam papers I could not understand and feeling a cold winding-sheet being drawn over the lifeless face of my future.

Each evening after supper some of the prefects would sit in the common room, puffing earnestly on pipes and discussing the day's papers, while the radio played The Byrds' 'Hey Mr Tambourine Man', The Beatles' 'Ticket to Ride' and Sandie Shaw's 'Long Long Live Love'. Others were off on the high jinks that were equally known to most of the school as they were unsuspected by the teaching staff. I sat and brooded virtuously, aware of failure gathering before me. I had no idea of the real disaster ahead.

ON THE VERY LAST Friday of my schooldays the prefects were taken out to dinner in a local restaurant, where we all – predictably – had Steak Diane. I was sitting next to Dave Ploughman. His latest obsession was Bob Dylan, and he knew all 283 verses of 'Maggie's Farm', which he sang with a happy drunken raucousness on the bus on the way back to Ratcliffe. As we drove up the driveway, I hoped we would stay in touch.

Thus to the final Sunday of the term, and the last of the weekly prefects' meetings, which was presided over, as usual in silence, by Father Nann. Stuart Morecambe made his farewell address, summarizing the year, and to my complete amazement, he let rip. He declared that most prefects had let the school down. We were irresponsible layabouts, who even dressed badly. Was it surprising that the boys were able to exploit our weakness? Ratcliffe's morale had suffered badly because of us. If it hadn't been for Father Nann and a handful of diligent prefects around him, the school would surely have gone to the dogs.

I've been to a few odious lectures in my life since then, but none has matched this one in such gratuitous hypocrisy. Then Nann weighed in, declaring that he had not previously been aware of these problems, but he fully understood and sympathized with the head prefect's silence hitherto on the matter. Stuart's undeserved loyalty to his subordinates did him credit. The school should be grateful for his honest analysis. He rose and left.

'What did you think of that?' I asked Bernie Keegan.

'Disgusting,' he said. 'Absolutely bloody disgusting.'

I went to my room and thought about Morecambe's speech, and the state of Ratcliffe. I still had wretchedly simple notions about school traditions and loyalty. I was also deeply aware of the profound taboos on 'snitching' and 'licking'. Yet equally, I was sure that Ratcliffe could soon be in ruins. I had failed as a firemen; surely I could not fail as a prefect. Had not my older brothers had triumphant careers here? I had been a failure. The least I could to was to save the school in which, at unspeakable expense to my mother, my younger brother Johnny was following. My duty was clear: to rescue Ratcliffe, without jeopardizing Morecambe and his associates. At around 10 pm, I went down to Nann's office.

'May I talk to you, Father?'

'Of course, Myers, come in. What is it?'

'I want to speak to you privately. As if this were in the confessional.'

'Do you wish me to hear your confession?'

'No, Father, not my confession. I need to talk to you.'

'Sit down, please.'

'Thank you, Father. I want to talk to you confidentially.'

He looked at me with those unwaveringly handsome eyes.

'I know you to be a young man with extreme sensitivity of conscience over the confession. It does you credit. But you cannot impose confessional rules on non-confessional matters. So what precisely do you want?'

'What I want is the assurance that no one might suffer from what I want to tell you – but you need to know, for the school's sake.'

'Why would anyone suffer?'

'Rules have been broken. You might even want to expel someone. And I couldn't allow that to happen.'

Nann looked at me and smiled wryly. 'The school year is over. No one is going to be expelled now, I can absolutely assure you on that. What would be the point?' *I can absolutely assure you on that.* That was exactly what I needed.

'And what I might tell you goes no further?'

'Yes, I can reasonably promise you that.'

'Thank you, Father. This is the position. The entire prefect system has broken down, and all the boys know it, but you obviously don't.'

'I see. But aren't you just echoing Morecambe earlier this evening?'

'No, Father. I'm saying something a little different. But I'm not saying anything more unless you guarantee no harm will come to anyone.'

He thought for a moment or two. 'I can certainly give you that guarantee.'

'There are some prefects who operate completely outside the school rules. They're selling cigarettes to boys, they permit certain boys to smoke, they're selling pornography and alcohol, and almost the entire school knows this. You know what a torrid time we've had with the fifth form. Now you know why. It's almost impossible to maintain order with all this going on. Next year, things will probably be far worse.'

He was looking at me in astonishment. 'Who's behind this?'

'I'll tell you no names. The purpose of my visit isn't to cause anyone any trouble. The reason I'm telling you this is so you can start with a clean slate next year.'

'But I am head of senior school, and prefect of discipline. I must have names!'

'I'm sorry, Father, but I can and will give you none.'

'But at least tell me the name of the ringleader. I can guarantee no harm will come to him.'

'No, Father, I told you, I'll give you no names.'

'But you can tell me who is not involved. That's the least you can do.'

'No, Father, I can't do that.'

'But this is preposterous. Someone like Keegan couldn't possibly be involved in this.'

'No, Keegan is not involved.'

At that moment, I knew I had blundered.

'I see. And who else is innocent, apart from yourself?'

'I'm sorry, Father, I told you the purpose of this visit isn't to start an inquiry into the past, but to prevent the same thing happening next year. I could've waited till after I'd left the school and written to you, but I just wanted to tell you now, in person, to show you how serious I am.'

'Your scruples do you credit: but surely, you cannot expect …'

'Father, you gave me your word …'

'Yes, yes, of course. But as you know, this has not been a confession.'

I left, knowing that I had made a serious blunder in giving Nann even one name. I'd speak to Keegan first thing tomorrow.

Nann was, as usual, presiding at the breakfast table the next morning, though now looking somewhat more haggard and distracted than usual. He did not engage Morecambe in the regular morning chatter. Sitting just down from me and on the same side of the long prefects' table, and therefore invisible, was Bernie Keegan. It was Monday, a day for packing. Tuesday's last hour after breakfast would be spent in final farewells as another generation of boys set out for the world.

I went over to Bernie as we left the refectory and began to tell him what had happened the previous night. He cut me short. 'So it was you. I should have guessed. Nann called me to his study last night. He said he knew about what was going on amongst the prefects. He asked me if it was true. I said it was.'

'Oh fuck! You didn't tell him who was involved?'

'Of course not. He just asked who definitely wasn't involved. Actually, I said you.'

'Anyone else?'

'No. No one. Except Freddie.' Jesus Christ Almighty. Freddie, the clueless Boer moron who couldn't fool his own dog.

'You told him Freddie?'

Bernie blinked idiotically. 'I was tired.'

'Christ. We've got to get to him.'

We raced to his room, but there was no sign of him. He hadn't made his bed, which was standard and mandatory procedure for all boys, even prefects, directly after breakfast. So Nann had got to him as he left the ref. We waited. Finally, the gormless son of the Broederbond came down the corridor, his wide Afrikaaner face blessed as always with a sublime look of utter stupidity. 'Guys,' he said. 'Wow, am I glad to see you. That Nann fellow, he's been giving me such a bloody grilling.'

'Freddie. Listen. Did you give him any names?'

'Sure. But only of the boys who I'm sure weren't involved.'

My heart folded within me. 'How many names did you give him?'

'Half a dozen. Maybe more. But it's all right. I didn't rat on anyone.'

'Freddie ... oh, it doesn't matter.'

I went to my room to do my packing, knowing that everything was now out of control. Nann was going to get to the bottom of this – the only consolation was that he had given me his word that there would be no consequences for anyone. Soon afterwards, one of the 'innocent' prefects came to my door. Father Nann would like to see me now. I went directly, sick with terror. He welcomed me coldly, and this time did not invite me to sit.

'You have behaved with some degree of responsibility in this affair. However, I believe there's more to this than meets the eye. I have the names of some boys who were deeply implicated in the corruption at the heart of this school. I want you to tell me the names you know.'

'You already know that I won't do that.'

'I'm not giving you any choice in the matter. Unless you hand over those names, I must regard you as complicit in this affair.'

For the first time in my life, but not the last, I felt the reptile of calculated betrayal place its leathery tentacles around my throat.

'Complicit? But it was me who told you about it in the first place. And why are you trying to get names? You can't do anything about it anyway. You promised. You gave me a guarantee!'

'No, I didn't. I merely said, "I can give you a guarantee." I didn't actually give the guarantee. That is known as moral reservation, which you should know about, because it was I who taught you about it. And even without that, a promise given on false premises is not binding.'

'What false premises?'

'What false premises? You concealed your role in the midnight swim. What else have you concealed?'

The midnight swim. That meant Martin had ratted on me. Richard, not being a prefect, wouldn't yet have been interrogated.

'The swim was just a swim. There wasn't anything else.'

'Nothing sexual?'

'Absolutely not.' My tone convinced him. So, I had finally some reason to be grateful for my sexual failure.

'Very well. Either way, the matter is now out of my hands.'

'Sorry, Father, but what does that mean?'

'Well, since you misled me, whatever undertakings I might

have given are now null and void. Father Morris is waiting for you in his study.'

Father Morris? Fuck me.

That serpent was indeed waiting for me in the perpetually dark, book-lined icebox from which he ruled his little empire, the skin on his thin temples wan and pulsing, as if his cranium had been removed to allow his brain more room for malice. 'You're in serious trouble, Myers, you know that, don't you? You've entered a conspiracy with other boys, which you have now chosen to inform on, no doubt in a pathetic attempt to save yourself. I have a list of boys due to be expelled before me. Your name will be added to the list unless you cooperate fully.'

Giddy with vertigo, disbelief and anger, I struggled for words. 'I was in no conspiracy. Father Nann gave me his word that nothing would happen to the boys involved.'

'Lying will not get you out of this pickle you're in. Father Nann trusted you. He didn't realize what you were up to.'

'Father, I was up to nothing.'

'Ha! These are the boys who are going to be expelled: Ploughman, O'Malley, Gardiner, Kavanagh and Stanley.'

'But you can't, Father. A promise was made. The term is over.'

'Don't you come bursting into my office, telling me what I can or can't do. The question is, shall your name be added to the list?'

I stayed silent at this point, and he dismissed me from his office. I went to the prefects' common room. The 'guilty' parties were not present. Those who were all stayed silent. The only one I could trust was Bernie Keegan. I called him outside.

'They've got the names,' I told him.

'They didn't bloody well get them from me,' he said. 'What's going to happen?'

'Christ … I think they're going to get the chop.'

'Fuck me. This is the last day. They can't do that, can they?'

'There's no point,' I said, reconsidering. 'It would be just too vindictive. They're trying to scare us.'

'Trying to? They may as well stop now, because in my case, they've already fucking well succeeded.'

That evening we sat in silence in the common room, eighteen-year-old boys in the final hours of our school days, As it approached 10 pm we said goodnight for the last time ever. It was still light outside.

There was a deathly hush in the refectory at breakfast time. Nobody ate. Five places at the prefects' table were unfilled. Once the meal was done, so too would the term, as would my time as a schoolboy. Nann rang the refectory bell and rose.

'I would normally say farewell to the upper school at this point, because you'd be going home directly we've finished. But this morning is different. The headmaster has called a special assembly, and you're all to be in there in ten minutes. You may leave breakfast from this point.'

The entire school had already gathered in an ominous silence in the assembly hall when Morris strode in at a minute before nine. He didn't need to call us to order. This was a firing squad and we all knew it.

He announced these were grave times. A handful of prefects had brought disgrace on the school. Such future behaviour would never again be tolerated. To ensure this was so, all the culprits were going to be expelled. Then he named the boys, one by one, like a list of fatal diseases. That done, he left, his black cassock swirling silently in his slipstream.

The boys of Ratcliffe stood, stunned, for a long while, before wordlessly dispersing. I went to my room to get my cases. There was a knock on the door. I opened it. Standing there was Dave Ploughman.

'I came to say goodbye,' he said.

'Oh Dave,' I said, nearly in tears. 'I am so very, very sorry.'

'Fuck me. I don't know what'll become of me now. Dad will fucking kill me. I might lose my college place. I've no idea. There'll be hell at home. My poor mother …' Then this big soft giant sobbed. Expulsion. The one great taboo.

Of course, he didn't know that I was the innocent instigator of all this. Only Bernie, Nann, Morris and possibly Freddie did. And almost alone of all the 'innocent' prefects, I had given absolutely no names. But I still felt thoroughly disgusted with myself – as well I might, and as well I do.

'Goodbye, Kevin,' he said, offering me his hand.

'Goodbye, Dave,' I said, taking it.

With that handshake, he passed from my life forever.

I was quite incoherent when Mum came to collect me shortly afterwards. There had been no fond farewells and promises to stay in touch to mark the end of our schooldays, just a surly air of unspoken recrimination and general accusation over an entire year of departing students. I told her of the expulsions, but not of my role in causing them. Mine was the disgust and shame of an inadvertent betrayer advertently betrayed.

I went looking for work. The only job I could find was as a council street sweeper, rising at six to be in the depot at seven. It was dire work, but it was all I was suited for. My final school report came, written and signed by Jack Morris. It read: 'Kevin is a nice enough young man, and not without a certain integrity, but frankly, his limited intellectual talents suggest that a largely unpromising future awaits him.'

Two other students were on my street-sweeping gang. We knew one morning from the newspapers that our exam results would have arrived while we were at work. A prematurely autumn chill already lay in the early air when we met the following day. They both got three As, and places at Oxford and Cambridge. I had three fails.

My life was now at a dead end. Barely more than two years before, the question was, which subject would I be first in? Now, I was a complete failure in all regards. But at least my terrible school secret was safe.

A couple of days later, the phone rang and Mum took it in her bedroom. 'It's for you,' she called. This was unusual, for no one ever phoned me. I went to her room and took the call. The September sunlight was cascading through the gauze of her windows. It was John O'Malley. His voice was cold and purposeful.

'My father is on the board of governors of Ratcliffe, as you probably know. He refused to accept that I could be expelled just like that, so he went to Jack Morris, and asked for the name of the person who had blown the whistle. And Morris told him it was a fair request. So Morris named you as the informer who gave us all away. Look. I'm not going to abuse you. There's no point. I just want to thank you for ruining my life.' He rang off.

John vanished from my life forever, as did the other expelled boys in this story. All I know is that after a lifetime of very visible sadness, he died relatively young. I see the name of one of them occasionally – he is a Queen's Counsel in London. As for the rest, I do not know what happened to them. But as for the meaning of deep and abiding guilt, to this very day, I know that all too well.

Fourteen

I BEGAN to study fresh A Levels at Charles Keene Technical College in Leicester, choosing history and economic history, confirming how little my brain was functioning. For even good results in two such closely related topics could not possibly get me a place in any British university. The irony was perfect: the college had been designed to move working-class students up the hierarchy, not rescue middle-class students from plummeting in the opposite direction. The apple trees in New Way Road were bountiful that autumn, and Mum put the fruit on the kitchen windowsill. Whenever I have since smelled that rare combination of acetone mingling with the sweet silicates of furniture polish I have been almost overpowered by a terrible sense of helplessness and failure.

Dave Ploughman's personal legacy to me lived on in my musical tastes. Over the coming months, Count Basie's and Woodie Herman's bands came to the De Montfort Hall in Leicester and I attended both concerts. I told my mother I was meeting friends there, but how could I do that when I had none? I went alone, and sat alone and left alone and went home alone, a sorry echo of my father's trips to Filbert Street.

I was little better at Charles Keene than I had been at Ratcliffe. I got through the lectures and wrote my papers and no one thought very highly of me. I lived with Mum and whatever paying guest was in the spare room. Maggy was studying English in Birmingham, where she rapidly found many friends. On Saturday afternoons I briefly played hockey for a local club but couldn't afford the weekly fees. And anyway, the half-dozen matches I played hadn't opened up any social vistas for me. I caught a bus home after each game and watched television with Mum, another wild teenage Saturday night in the swinging sixties.

One Wednesday night, I went to a folk club. I drank Coke, mostly because I didn't like the taste of alcohol, but also because I had no money. A blonde girl rather tentatively approached me during the break.

'Are you Kevin Myers?'

'Yes,' I said cautiously. 'I'm sorry. Do we know one another?'

'We used to, when I was a kid. Me dad ran the off-licence at the top of Buckminster Road. I'm Beverley.' I remembered her. She would sometimes serve me when I would go and buy a bottle of Guinness for Dad. Then she was a little girl, but now she was a young woman, very blonde, with flaxen eyebrows and enchantingly large breasts. 'I thought you wouldn't remember me ... you being so posh and everything, all stuck up.'

'Oh, I'm not stuck up.'

'We all used to look at the doctor's children playing on the roof of your garage. We used to think you were very grand.'

She introduced her friend Leslie to me. 'This is Kevin. He used to be dead posh. But he says he's not posh any more.'

The new girl smiled. 'Are you dead posh or not?'

'No, not dead posh. Not posh at all.'

'You speak real posh. Where'd you go to school?'

'A place called Ratcliffe.'

'Ratcliffe College? That's real posh, that is, isn't it Beverley?'

'Course it is. Didn't you used to go to Wyggeston?'

She pronounced it Wigston.

'I did for a bit, then they sent me away to boarding school.'

'Then they sent me away to boarding school,' teased Beverley, in a facsimile of my accent. The other girl laughed, but nicely. I liked them both, but I was in a quandary. How could I chat up just one of them? Later I walked them to their bus stop, and then went to mine.

Thereafter, I would see them each Wednesday. Frankly, I really didn't care which one I got. They were both nice and both attractive, and both seemed to like me.

'You wouldn't want to meet us if you were with your school chums, would you?' said Leslie one evening. 'Us talking with Leicester accents and all.'

'That's not true,' I said hotly, but though inwardly, I wasn't so sure. I was a little bit of a snob, but also a little ashamed of my class-consciousness; the conflicted emotions that make the English middle classes so desperately insecure. But there was also a third, and almost physically disabling force at work – libido. I was desperate for a girlfriend, and on balance, Leslie seemed to be more interested in me. However, I still hadn't worked out how to sunder these socially conjoined girls when my first term at Charles Keene ended and I managed to get a job at Lewis's department store again. And on my first day, in the staff canteen, sitting by herself, I saw Leslie.

Delighted to catch her alone, I went over and greeted her warmly, before sitting down opposite her. She looked at me briefly, said nothing, rose and left. It took me a moment to grasp my mistake. I'd taken her by surprise. She'd seen me completely out of my usual context, and so hadn't recognized me. So the next day, I returned to the canteen, at the same time, and there was she was again. I calmly went over to her. 'It's Leslie, isn't it? Hello. I'm Kevin Myers. We met at the folk club. You were with Beverley, remember?'

She looked askance at me, rose, and walked away. What was going on? I decided to find out where she worked, and finally found her sitting behind the counter in the foreign tours section, talking to a couple of fellow employees. Taking a deep breath, I walked over to her counter. She looked briefly at me, then turned, whispered something to her two companions, and all three got up and left in protective convoy. Why should a girl who had always seemed so nice now be treating me so awfully? I felt baffled, angry and humiliated.

The next day, during a break, I was standing at the sweets area in the basement. 'Kevin? Hello?'

It was Leslie again, this time, apparently, very pleased to meet me. I was not, and still am not, a quick thinker in unexpected social circumstances, but on this occasion my mind instantly invented the required strategy. I stared at her with mounting puzzlement on my face.

She repeated, 'Kevin? Remember me?'

I said nothing, but continued to study her with I hoped was a look of bewildered disdain.

'Kevin? The folk club?'

I shook my head and turned away, though I could see her face out of the corner of my eye. The tactic proved to be gratifyingly effective, because Leslie actually looked really hurt and surprised.

'There! I said all along that, deep down, you'd think I wasn't good enough for the likes of you.'

'Well now, it looks like you were right then, weren't you?' I looked at her briefly. She was in tears. Good. I walked away, my heart lifting with triumph. My plan had worked. It is never good to hurt someone gratuitously, but this was so thoroughly deserved. I also knew now what to do next to deliver the coup de grace. I would race to her department and leave a note, telling her that she was not to approach me anymore.

As I approached the foreign tours department on the fourth floor, I saw Leslie already sitting there, but now with different clothes from those she'd been wearing a couple of moments ago.

Pincers of very cold steel began to close about my heart. A floor manager whom I vaguely knew was standing nearby.

'Who's that girl over there?' I asked him.

'Luciana? The manager's niece? A right little cúnt, pardon the French, only she's Italian, over 'ere to learn English, but the only ones she'll ever bloody speak to are them folk in foreign tours what speak her lingo.'

Two girls. One face. And the girl whom I really liked, and wanted to like me, was the one I had just so ruthlessly and catastrophically snubbed. I ran over to the lifts. Gone. I raced to the stairs and toppled down them, rubber legs flopping beneath me, violently barging customers out of the way. I reached confectionery, and sprinted around the various counters, but of Leslie there was no sign. She was already gone: gone from the basement, gone from Lewis's, and as I was to discover over the next few Wednesdays in the folk club, which I haunted with a quite sepulchral persistence, gone – along with Beverley – for ever from my life.

I had remained in touch with Richard and accepted an invitation to stay with him and his family. I set off to hitchhike to Brighton from Leicester, and at a motorway service station near Luton got a lift in the back of a windowless van full of oily engine parts. Another hitchhiker was already squatting invisibly in the dark; he spoke loudly to us, and indeed to anyone else within a hundred yards, of his time working in a holiday camp in Skegness.

'Bloomin' great, Bútlins,' he roared happily, 'all the fúckin' bint you could fúckin' want. Married, teenage, the lot. Ah were shaggin' a different fúckin' bird every blúddy night, and maybe shaggin' their mams the next mornin'. "oliday camps? Ah fúckin' lúv 'em.'

I was eighteen and a half. At Ratcliffe, I had once kissed a girl, and briefly stolen a feel of a nipple before she had pushed my hand away: that was the extent of my sexual experience. This boy sounded as if he were around my age, but seemed to have spent his entire teenage years in a ceaseless riot of dissolution and debauchery.

'Eh úp, driver! You know wa' rappens in 'oliday camps, every fúckin' night? It's fúckin' grea'! The 'usbands goo off and get drunk while the wives play bingo. Dead easy, mate. At the break, wen they goo aht to 'ave a Vimto an' crisps, you cha'rum up, pu' rem again a wall, tek their knickers off and Bob's your fúcking úncle. 'oliday camps? Ah fúckin' lúv 'em!'

In Trafalgar Square in London, I slowly and uncomfortably unknotted my limbs and managed to dismount from the back of the van into broad and surprising daylight. I squinted at my Lothario companion. His face was strangely unchanged from our schooldays' encounters. 'I know you. You're Edward Warwick!'

'Oo ya beauty! So oo the fúck are you?'

'Oh, no one you'd remember.'

'Fúck off. Betcher ah fúckin' do.'

I told him. He didn't. I went on to Brighton to stay with Richard for a couple of days. It was there he told me more about Brother O'Dwyer, who had been sexually abusing him. 'He got at Montmorency, night after night, apparently far worse than with me.'

Dear God almighty: the innocent little French boy whose father had sent him to Ratcliffe out of admiration for all things British. O'Dwyer had been sacked, and the scandal hushed up, though quite how the Montmorency family had been squared away was not part of Richard's story. 'Anyway, that sort of stuff is all behind me now,' adding that he now had a quite wonderful girlfriend, with whom he was having full sex. 'Cunts are the loveliest softest things,' he said. 'So soft. When you touch one, you simply won't believe it.'

Well, that much was certainly true. Either way, my days of unconsummated dalliance with homosexuality were truly gone.

THE FOLLOWING May I sat my second batch of A Levels and got two poor passes. I was in the funnel of failure, heading downwards. I had neither personal skills nor academic ones, and I can't imagine how Mum managed to live with me. And it was she who then had a brainwave. In her younger days in Dublin she had known Jeremiah Hogan, then a young academic and now President of University College Dublin. She wrote to him, asking if UCD might possibly have some places put aside for Irish exiles.

That was the summer England won the World Cup. The day after the victory Bill drove Johnny and me to the ferry, and, leaving the car there, we travelled to Ireland. On a Dublin city centre bus, the conductor, upon hearing our accents, asked us where we were from.

'Leicester,' I said.

The woman in front of us turned round. 'My brother's in Leicester. Maybe you know him ... Jimmy Ryan. From Tipperary originally, like myself.'

'I've a cousin in Leicester,' chimed in another passenger. 'Seamus Patterson. Very quiet place, he says.'

'Nice people, Leicester people,' added someone else.

'Gordon Banks plays for Leicester,' observed someone else.

'Wasn't the World Cup fantastic?' said another voice. There was a general murmur of approval. We were now the subject of a general topic of conversation amongst the passengers: nothing as spontaneous or warm or hospitable had ever happened in Leicester. More amazing things were to follow. Uncle Jim, a bank manager in Naas, twenty miles outside Dublin, with insane generosity, insisted we borrow his car for the duration of our holiday.

On my return to Leicester I found a miracle taking shape. Jeremiah Hogan of UCD had replied, suggesting that I apply for a place in the quota for foreign students. I immediately did so. And though this was year of the baby boomers, UCD's foreign quota was, incredibly, still unfilled. All over the western world, universities had waiting lists in all categories, but UCD had a couple of spare places in the only category for which I was suited – a foreign student in the social studies department. Thus it was that Ireland, which had once rejected and nearly ruined my father, had thrown me a lifeline just as I was about to slip down the silicate sides of life's crevasse into complete and utter failure.

Fifteen

THE IRELAND that I found on arrival in UCD was not the Ireland that I glimpsed before in childhood, nor was it in any sense the Ireland that was to emerge in the coming decades. It was largely joyless, grey, repressed, its cultural hues reflected in the dying Georgian architecture and its cold wet streets. I was not a confident student, and hid my own deep sense of inadequacy behind a facade of brusqueness, sarcasm and arrogance.

I have to say, with the advantage of years, that some of these qualities were fully merited by what I found in Dublin. Half a century of independence had created a dreary, isolated backwater, whose cultural tropes were the creation of the censor, not of the artist. The first Irish film censor, an idiot named Montgomery, had in the first seventeen years of self-government banned 1903 films. By 1954, just twelve years before I arrived in Dublin, an Irish minister actually boasted in the Dáil that at that moment, 5400 books were banned. By the end of the year, the figure was closer to 6000.

Moreover, UCD had none of the intellectual energy or curiosity that I had expected, not least from my reading of Flann O'Brien's novel, *At Swim-Two-Birds*, some of which was set in the college in the 1930s. My attempts to discuss it were rebuffed by the stout walls of ignorance: no one else appeared to have read it. My manners did not win friends amongst most of the thin-skinned Irish students, though some of the sturdier Americans found me moderately tolerable, as too did my aunts and uncles, whose happy greetings wherever I turned up at their doors were as unmerited as they were welcome.

Nothing of moment distinguished my eventless first year. I was deeply, deeply unhappy, a creature maimed by grief, guilt, self-doubt, and the weird dementia of unsatisfied lust. In any year, there are 8760 hours. It seems I spent at least 8000 of those completely alone, in unconfined solitary confinement, gazing at the grey ceiling of my tiny bedsitter in Harcourt Street, dwelling on the fate that had befallen poor Dad, and that other fate that had struck my schoolfriends, to which I had been an indispensable accomplice. Happiness was a remote and exotic archipelago, away from which the currents of life seemed to be perpetually driving me. Loneliness is often an industrious mason, ceaselessly creating fresh prison walls.

A nice American, Irene, who had taken pity on me quite early on at the end of the academic year, brought her mother round to say hello before leaving on a tour of Europe, then home to Washington State. 'Let me give you my address,' she said, 'lest you ever come to the States.'

'Thanks, that won't be necessary. I don't plan to visit Washington.'

Kindly Irene stood stricken, crestfallen. Her mother's eyebrows knitted in silent rage at the needless insult done to her daughter. Wordlessly they departed, like moons fleeing my planet of sourness.

That summer I hitchhiked across Europe. In Switzerland I was given a lift by Glen, an American, in the brand-new Rover 2000 that he had bought directly from the factory in Solihull. He decided to stay on a campsite, and there he rented a tent, but he allowed me to sleep in his Rover. One doesn't 'sleep' in a car so much as discover the many acute angles of insomniac discomfort and early onset arthritis that a car seat makes possible. So finally I lay down beside his Rover and slept in the outdoors. I found I liked sleeping in the open air.

In the morning I went to the unisex showers, at that time, a truly exotic concept. After a glorious deluge that washed my accumulated filth away, as I turned off the shower, the soap slipped from my hand. Looking down, I noticed that the water on the floor was now a perfect mirror, not merely within my cubicle, but also, via the partition that ended about a foot from the floor, for the one beside me. At that moment, a woman walked into that shower cubicle, took off her gown, and draped it over the door. She didn't immediately turn on the shower, but instead, began to masturbate. I watched, entranced by this most perfect and beautiful image beneath me. I could see nothing of her face, just her knees, thighs, her hand and her vulva. Did she realize I could see her? I have no idea. I stayed watching, motionless, until finally she convulsed, then turned on the shower. The image at my feet instantly vanished like a television screen having a white-out.

I did not emulate her. I merely turned on the cold shower to kill my own arousal. By the time I emerged from the shower, the mystery woman was gone forever. I dressed and left, richer in the knowledge of the appetites that drive us all, and how most of us sooner or later quell them alone. Such is not human failure, but how humans actually are.

Glen drove me to Lake Geneva. We sat at a pavement café and ate fresh green beans lightly fried in garlic butter, alongside the silver shimmering waters and beneath a perfect cerulean sky. A white Mark I Ford Mustang convertible drew up beside the lakeshore and halted. The driver and his blonde girlfriend remained sitting, listening to the opening bars of 'A Whiter Shade of Pale', and the music rang loudly over the café and glittering, murmuring waters. It was a moment from film: song and scene and setting seamlessly edited together, and I was the hero of this particular tale. For this was me, beside Lake Geneva, surrounded by rich, beautiful people, with a backing track of one of the most imperishable pieces of music that popular culture has ever devised. Not long before, I had watched a woman bring herself off. Synchronicity differs from mere coincidence when events become connected by little drawbridges, suddenly falling into place to create a narrative. That cinematic morning, I sensed the world inside me – my personal world, with its many radio telescopes and its sensors gazing longingly into the unknowns of outer space – slightly alter its focus. The grief of four years began to shift.

Everywhere I went, I heard The Beatles' 'All You Need Is Love', 'Lucy in the Sky With Diamonds', 'A Day in the Life' and the other tracks from *Sergeant Pepper*, plus Scott McKenzie's 'San Francisco'. In Matala in Crete, we new semi-hippies created a semi-commune in the ancient burial caves, which we treated with quite scandalous disrespect. They had been there for many hundreds of years: we youngsters destroyed them all that summer, while the locals looked on in silent rage, made impotent by the tyranny of a military government determined to encourage tourists, even of cool, unprincipled parasites like us. Thus was the Greek summer of love made possible by the Aegean junta. The downfall of the hippy phenomenon began, like all things, at the very moment of its birth.

We smoked dope, and we listened to the Beatles again and again and again, and to Gregorian plainchant, again and again and again. A Jewish girl from Minnesota called Beatrice confided that she was on the pill, and meaningfully left it that, and though too scared to act, I was sufficiently flattered and fortified for the next occasion. It duly came when a girl named Judith from Chicago (also Jewish), with the Matala starlight on my back and the Matala sand on hers, relieved me of a burden that I thought would be mine until granite was finally laid upon my sorry bones. It was memorable only for that, though of course poor Judith did not even have that consolation.

She woke me at dawn, shortly before she left to catch the early bus to Iraklion. I said we'd meet again at her hotel in Athens.

'Promise?' she said. 'You know, I really, really got to teach you a few basic things.'

'I promise. Wait a minute. I'll never remember the name of the hotel.'

I opened my rucksack and took out my new but already battered Penguin edition of Dostoyevsky's *Crime and Punishment*. 'Here,' I said. 'Write the address on this.'

'Don't let me down,' she said, scribbling the details on the frontispiece. She put the book down beside me, kissing my lips as she briefly fondled me in my sleeping bag. Athens was certainly something to look forward to.

'I won't. I promise.'

'Promises, shlomises. You guys.'

I stayed on, befriending other youngsters from across the USA, England, Scandinavia and Holland. There was one Irishman there, just one, called Derek, who playing to the stereotype, got drunk and punched an elderly Cretan in the beach bar. A huge Dutchman laid him out cold. That should have taught me that even boundless licence must have boundaries, but I was young, and remained determined to explore the emerging freedoms of my generation. I ate fried fish and drank retsina and ouzo and grew blacker and blacker in the African sun of Matala, the very summer that Joni Mitchell wrote her paean to that place. Was she there when I was?

Then it was time to move on, urgently, for I had an appointment in Athens with the luscious Judith. Just think: a hotel, a room, and light by which to examine her body with the molecular attention to detail that its contours, clefts and mounds so richly deserved. Four days after she left, I too I set off, fatally, not by bus, but hitching, and I soon got a lift on the back of a grape lorry. With an optimism that cannot even be explained by youth, on a vehicle that rattled and bucketed along a totally unmade road, I took out *Crime and Punishment* from my rucksack. The new-style Penguin paperbacks were bound with a particularly frangible glue. As my powers of concentration wrestled with the twin foes of Dostoyevskian moral complexity and the double-leaf suspension on a 1950s Opel truck, the Penguin spine suddenly cracked as if it had been hit by a broadsword. In a trice, the first fifty pages of the book broke free and whirled off in the slipstream, like a brood of feeding gulls panicked by a gunshot, taking with them, irretrievably into history, all of Judith's hotel details, and thus Judith also.

I returned from the giddy excitement of Europe to the grey austerity of Dublin to learn that I had done surprisingly well in my history exams. The department contacted me. Would I be prepared to study pure history, rather than the social science for which I had enrolled? It was even prepared to waive the usual requirement of first year French. Someone actually *wanted me*. Of course I said yes, and it was one of the wisest moves in my life.

This is not the place to record my relationship with the great teachers in the history department, men and women to whom I shall always be grateful. But that second year I was still not really connecting with the main body of Irish students. My friends were another bunch of Americans – Geraldine Hussey, Jack Rabuse, Ann Patterson, Gege Mackay, Jim Murphy, and others – and it was they who persuaded me to go the USA for the summer at the end of my second academic year.

Through the Union of Students in Ireland, I managed to arrange a job as camp counsellor at College Farm Settlement Camp at Willow Grove, outside Philadelphia. I was initially assigned to work with the older boys, aged fourteen to sixteen, but (as I later learnt) after just one meeting with me, Frank Jerome, the section leader, asked the Camp supervisor, Leonard C. Ferguson, to have me moved to a less sensitive area. He felt my manners were too abrupt and my language far too sarcastic for ghetto kids. But there was neither anyone else to take my place nor anywhere for me to go, so Frank, a cheery Italian-American, and his assistants Chuck, Martin and Roy would just have to put up with me. I wasn't liked initially, but spending every minute of my entire day with the boys enabled them to see past the facade of a sometimes brusque and disagreeable exterior. They even gave me a nickname, which is usually a sign of some regard. It was 'English', and was reasonably accurate as to my identity at the time.

Roy, one of my fellow counsellors, was black, as were half the boys, and about a third of those boys were a serious handful, including some who were certainly on their way to jail, or worse. The African-Americans (though that term hadn't yet come into use) were naturally drawn to Roy, despite the fact that he was a shallow, boastful creature. I didn't even try to win their support. One day, one of the black lads came to me.

'Hey, English,' he said. 'We got a problem we want you to sort out.'

I followed him to his hut, assuming that this 'problem' was between blacks and whites, and they wanted a white outsider, this 'English', partial to neither side, to arbitrate. But no, the disagreement was between two black groups. This was amazing: they preferred *my* judgment to Roy's.

Later I asked one of the boys why I had been chosen.

'You ain't so bad. Leastways, not as bad as you're tryin' to be.'

I grew to really like the boys, the blacks especially, and yes, I know that sounds patronizing, but that's the way it was. They were witty, sharp and, well, so naturally cool. Oddly enough, I think most of them came to like me also. Even more amazingly the 'R' word made its first appearance in my life. Respect. When a large black sixteen-year-old made some anti-Semitic remarks to a small Jewish boy, I challenged him.

'If you want to settle this outside with me, now, repeat what you just said.'

He didn't. My words were of course bluster. He was twice my size, and of course physical violence was totally outlawed. But far from the other black kids taking against me, they seemed to admire my stand against a bully they were all scared of. They admired me even more when I performed a cricket-style horizontal diving catch during a game of softball, so putting out the opposition's star batter. None of them had ever seen anything quite like that before. 'English' was suddenly a hero.

I knew I was having an impact when some white parents came to collect their son at the end of his stay. They had a present for me, aftershave called English Lime. 'He worships you,' confided his mother. 'He's had a bad time at school. No one's ever treated him with the respect that he says you've shown him. He even wants us to start calling him Kevin. We're so grateful.'

Not nearly as grateful as I was, less for the atrocious aftershave than for all the reasons that went into it. And that was how I was coming to perceive the American people: spontaneous generosity actually seemed to be a cultural characteristic. Over the coming weeks, my admiration for Americans intensified. I liked the forthrightness, the kindness, the transparency, the honesty, and most of all, the women. American girls had a frank openness that I had never found in England or Ireland.

'You want to go for a walk?' said one after meeting me during my first two days there before the campers had arrived. She took me to a chalet, where she turned and kissed me. We didn't do much more than that, but it was all very heartening. A nice Jewish girl called Ellen took a shine to me. One night we went for a walk in the fields, and it began to rain, hot tropical rain like I had never experienced before.

'Let's take our clothes off,' she whispered.

We did, and kissed, and rolled around in the grass, our naked flesh washed by the warm torrents of rainwater. We didn't have sex, just erotic sensual fun in the fizzing steaming boundless heavenly torrents. For a moment we were caught in headlights as a car rounded a distant bend. We froze. The lights swivelled on, and we collapsed with laughter in the lushly soaking meadow.

'I'm a virgin,' she told me later, as she lay on her back and I draped strands of warm wet grass over her naked body.

'We'll attend to that tomorrow,' I said, kissing her, and sure enough, we did. Not particularly successfully, but certainly within the meaning of the act. So: who can be surprised that I like Jewish girls?

Admittedly, I was still far too instantly and outwardly dismissive of those characteristics about the US that, without any thought or reflection, I found deeply uncool: the simplicity, the piety, the patriotism, virtues that I now deeply respect. But I was still just twenty-one, and a very young twenty-one. How could I be other than immature? Adult hormones had been carving a man from the green timber of my boyish frame and callow brain for only four years.

But now at least I was growing emotionally and gaining new friends, such as Larry Browning and his wife Jane. She was heartbreakingly beautiful, a dentist's daughter from Atlanta, and a natural patrician, a Dahomeyan princess of ancient pedigree. He was black also, though this was rather more of a cultural than chromatic or even racial concept, because he had strongly Caucasian features beneath a pale coffee complexion, rather like a high-caste Brazilian planter.

One day Larry was explaining to a group of us about the cultural difficulties for a black student like him in a largely white college.

'Black? You? You're not black,' I loudly scoffed, exaggerating my English accent. 'Give me a week in Greece, I'd be twice as black as you, and then nobody would have the least bloody idea which one round here was the genuine fucking nigger.'

The white counsellors' eyes opened wide in horror. But Jane clapped her hands delightedly, as she and Larry erupted with laughter. They instantly understood my dismissal of race as a defining concept in life. They liked me, and I really, really liked them. That was that.

At the end of my time in the camp I stayed in Danbury, Connecticut, with Jack Rabuse, and Tom Tessier, in New Haven, two of my American friends from UCD. And then with my rucksack on my back, I set off round the USA. These were genuinely fraught times for America. In the previous few months, Bobby Kennedy and Martin Luther King had been assassinated. At the Chicago Democratic Convention the police had decided that, after a full year of campus riots, it was now surely their turn to riot, as they joyfully beat protesters' skulls into a pulp. Many people on the East Coast doubted my sanity, travelling to the Midwest and California, especially looking as I did, with my long hair, scruffy jeans, and an old ex-army rucksack.

But there was never a better time to see America. My initial admiration of the country and its people grew to unbridled love. Though I must have been a truly weird sight, scruffily hitching across the great flatlands of the Midwest, I never wanted for lifts. I imagine all westward travellers find their hearts lifted by the first glimpse of the golden arch at St Louis. Mine certainly was, as it beckoned me on, towards the huge bridge over the Mississippi and the great beyond. As the brown waters beneath me toiled towards New Orleans, I was almost overwhelmed with happiness. My drivers were usually courteous and curious. Some would invite me to stay at their houses, and eat with their families, but for the most part I'd spend the night in fields, in my sleeping bag, covered in a huge plastic bag. Day by day and lift by lift, dusk by dusk and dawn by dawn, the load of the previous half decade was removed from my shoulders. In the course of my journey west, whatever happy, nice Kevin Myers that had been buried in a toxic silt of misery by Ratcliffe's betrayals and by Dad's death, gradually emerged once more, like a long-lost statue being exposed by a running tide. The best songs that summer were all British: 'Hey Jude', 'Those Were the Days My Friend', 'Just Help Yourself'. I followed the sun westward, and each evening I was gloriously blinded by golden sunset after golden sunset, luring me onward.

I hiked into Wyoming and the old badlands, Laramie and Medicine Bow, and even older badlands still, Como Bluff and Dinosaur Graveyard. There was no interstate there, just two-lane blacktops, winding their way through the clay-coloured sandstone bluffs and buttes. Men wore cowboy hats and stayed silent as they drove. In Colorado I got a lift from a one-legged ex-soldier who had trodden on a landmine in Tunisia in 1943. He was old enough to be my father, but we became instant friends. He bought me a meal at a hotel and talked about his life. A woman made eyes at him.

'You're in luck there,' I said.

'Got a wife at home,' he replied simply. 'And anyway, t'aint me she's looking at, it's you. Drink up. We got us some driving to do.'

Early the next morning he dropped me near Ogden in Utah, where I soon got a lift from an army helicopter pilot bound for Vietnam. He shamed me with his kindness and his genuine interest in my opposition to the war. When I had finished, he said: 'What'll happen to this world if the communists are allowed to take South Vietnam by force of arms and we just let them? Just ask the Czechs what they think.'

I had no answer to that. That summer Prague had been reconquered by Soviet forces. When we parted, I took photos of him, and he took some of me in his chopper helmet, which he said he'd forward to me from Vietnam. I gave him my address in Leicester. I knew him by this time. He would never not write if he could. We parted at Salt Lake City, me for my tour of his native land, of which I had already seen more than he had, and him for war. I never heard from him again.

I headed for San Francisco, intending to stay there, but first I wanted to go to San José, to stay with another American friend from Dublin, a former Marine called Jim Murphy. As my lift entered the city, sure enough, the Dionne Warwick song came on the radio, 'Do You Know the Way to San José?'

By God, I certainly did now.

Happiness flooded my soul, like sunlight pouring through a trap door into a roof-space. Freedom was everywhere, and it was all mine. One of Jim's friends was a cool Californian dude with a wide cowboy hat. We gatecrashed a wedding, where we drank champagne and smoked dope, and performed potentially lethal gambols on a trampoline. I did an enormous bounce, and coming down head first, missed the net completely, but hit my shoulder on the frame and so broke my fall. What might have been a snapped neck turned out to be three wedding gatecrashers lying on the lawn, laughing till the California night warmly fell.

Youth was mine. Joy was mine. The world was mine. And the life that I've had ever since could almost be said to have begun beside that trampoline, where it might well, another inch or two either way, have ended. Days later, outside San Diego, a Ford Falcon did a u-turn a couple of hundred yards after passing me, came back, did another u-turn just down the road, and then stopped beside me.

'Hop on in, son,' said the driver, leaning across his wife. 'Just put your bag beside you in the back there, trunk's full.'

Most cars in southern California were air-conditioned. Not this one. So we drove slowly, with the windows open. Over the next few hours, I learnt a bit about them. Their names were Gene and Irene Martin, from Tustin, California. They were in their fifties, I'd guess, but looked much older. They were originally from Oklahoma, and had got married in 1941, just before he was drafted: all in all, a bad year to be called up. He'd spent the entire war in the navy. 'Wadn't all bad. I ain't never learned to read nor right proper afore the navy got their hands on me.'

They'd tried hard for a child when he got home – as you would, I reckoned, after four years' separation, child-hungry or not – and sure enough, in due course a boy was born. Just the one.

'I wadn't goin' pick you up, you bein' a long-haired hippy an' all, only Ma here said you seemed the same age as our boy. She figured that maybe you weren't as bad as you looked, and I guess she was right.'

Their son had been living in San Diego when he'd been served with his draft papers. He'd been opposed to the war, and there had been big family rows over it. His father had argued that since he, the father, had done his bit for the USA, now it was his son's turn. So finally, the boy agreed. The previous month he'd been doing the rounds, just saying goodbye to his friends prior to departing for boot camp when his VW beetle was hit by a truck and he was killed outright.

'My, that hurt real bad,' remembered the old man in an odd, disconnected voice. His wife, half looking back at me, nodded: her fine thin face chiselled from the first stone ever to know the meaning of grief.

'Maybe God din't want him to go to no war,' she whispered; a meagre enough consolation, all things considered.

We were silent for a while as we drove through the foothills of the Chocolate Mountains of Southern California. And it got me thinking. My Dad had lived to over sixty, and had left six healthy children. And here was I, as free as any man on this wide earth, with no worries and my whole life before me. Other people's grief is an egregious price for wisdom, but sometimes it is the only available currency.

We travelled on through the day, and they spoke about their lives and their boy. It was almost as if he were still alive. Maybe the essence of such bereavement is the ritual calling up of the dead, day after day, until the cold dawn when one wakes and realizes that what one has is all that one has, and all that one must henceforth live with. And that moment had finally come for me.

When it came to the parting of the ways, we all got out of the Falcon. Their faces were gaunt, lined, hard-worked. I first shook Gene's gnarled hand. It was like shaking a hoof with leather fingers.

'Ain't never again goin' to judge no book by its doggone cover, no sir,' he said. He didn't smile, but there was real affection in his eyes.

Then I shook Irene's hand, while she stood stiff, aloof, her cotton summer dress hanging limply around her legs. Then I impulsively bent to kiss her. Coyly, she offered me her cheek, while Gene laughed approvingly. They drove away, leaving me with my rucksack in the Arizona grit, I never to forget them, their dignity and their fortitude. Whenever people grandly talk about 'Americans', that's the couple I like to bring to mind, and the boy I never knew.

Most of the best people I met were ardent patriots who supported the Vietnam War. I, of course, did not, and alas, I usually didn't spare my drivers my voluble opinions. However, these Americans were invariably gracious towards this arrogant and uppity outsider, and always wished me well. Each nightfall I made my bed in the scrub, away from the road. Once I woke with a snake in my sleeping bag, coiled against my warm stomach, its scales resting on the bare skin of abdomen. I lay there till the heat of the rising sun finally drove my guest away. That reptile was the only living creature I ever shared a night with during my long journey round America. But I didn't mind, not a bit – for I was free.

Arizona, New Mexico, Oklahoma, Texas, Arkansas, Louisiana: I wiped the dust of them all from my feet. My brother Bill was by chance working for a year at Loyola University in New Orleans, and after briefly staying, I made my way through Mississippi and Alabama to Georgia. I never had any problems getting lifts. I still prattled my opinions witlessly to all who would listen. On the interstate between Meridian and Tuscaloosa, a truck driver listened carefully to my voluble anti-war vapourings for a while, before crying out loud: 'You're durn right! We ain't got no business fighting them there Viet-nam-ese way over there in Asia somewheres. Why, we got our own Viet-nam right here at home, with them there fuckin' niggahs. It's the niggahs we should be napalming, yes sir, not them there fuckin' little Chinese gooks!'

Thereafter I tended to keep my anti-war opinions to myself. Wherever I went, I met only courtesy and friendliness. I would usually sleep in fields, which is how my face got infested with chiggers: tiny parasites that lay eggs beneath your facial skin, causing a delightful acne, which passes when the young hatch and depart. In Atlanta, Georgia, I stayed for a couple of days with Larry and Jane Browning, the absurdly beautiful couple I had befriended in College Farm Camp. The comfort of their apartment told me I'd had enough of living rough. I got a Greyhound bus to New York and from there caught another to Danbury, Connecticut, arriving there at 2 am. The town was dark and dead, save for an all-night Dunkin' Doughnuts near the depot. I went in and rang Jack Rabuse and then ordered a Coke and a ring of deep-fried dough that tasted of plastic and engine oil. In the neon-lit pall, the air-conditioner purred and single men wordlessly stirred their coffee, as loneliness sounded its silent tocsin to all save me. On the road, a new man had been born, and that man had happiness for a friend.

I stayed with the Rabuses for a couple of days, and I still regret not asking Jack's father about his war-time service in the USAAF, of which he was immensely proud. Chances come, linger briefly in the half-light by the door, and unless invited in, vanish forever. A week later I was back in Ireland, completely transformed, just as the copycat virus of student insurrection arrived in UCD from Paris and Berkeley. Within months I was to become the foremost troublemaker of my year, no doubt causing poor Jeremiah Hogan to clutch his temples in disbelief that his kindness had been so ill-rewarded. Yet for all that, I was a nicer youngster, and in my new persona I had mysteriously acquired a public charisma, which enabled me to speak well and to hold audiences. I talked much undergraduate gibberish, of course. I remember one line before an enraptured crowd: 'Universities are meant to be bastions of democracy, whereas this wretched place is the last bastion of a decrepit gerontocracy.'

This witless rodomontade got a roar of approval that afternoon, and a rather more personal endorsement from a little redhead that night.

In all the tumult of that final year I was expecting to fail my finals, but instead I took a first in pure history, the only one of the year. Within a further eighteen months I had landed a job as a reporter with RTÉ in the Belfast newsroom, as the Northern Ireland Troubles lurched towards catastrophe. And though in one sense it was the USA that had transformed me, the trajectory of my adult life had begun earlier. The launchpad had been Dad's death, and the resulting calamity had taken me to a life in that unexpected planet called Ireland, which had effectively expelled Dad all those years before.

Epilogue

I SPENT seven years in Belfast, which I describe in my memoir, *Watching the Door*. Many factors then caused me to leave, but one event I did not relate occurred in London, where Jeananne Crowley, an old college friend and actress, was living. She had asked me to take a break from Belfast, and so I did. I knew that Jeananne's landlord was a solicitor called Bernie, and that his household at Sotheby Road, Highbury, was easy-going and semi-communal.

Soon after my arrival, Bernie returned home. He was about six years older than me, and looked strangely familiar.

'Are you a Londoner?' I asked.

'No, actually, I'm from Leicester,' he said pleasantly.

I paused, as his full name came back to me. Then I examined my memory bank, before studying him carefully, with what I hoped was a look of Holmesian deductiveness.

'You're Jewish, I think,' I said in a measured voice, 'and you went to – yes, Wyggeston Grammar School, where you studied classics at A Level, largely under a sarcastic old bastard … Wilcox, was it? And you were a prefect, and during morning assembly you used to be in charge of the Catholics and Jews outside during prayers. The Jews were a well-behaved lot generally, but you had to protect a Catholic boy called Warwick from the most violent boy in the school, a Jew called Spielberg, and though he was lazy and violent, Spielberg managed to get nine grade As at O Level.'

Bernie sat there with his jaw open. He finally managed to speak.

'Good God! Can you tell all that just from looking at me?'

'In part, yes. But also because I was one of those little boys. Not a Jew, however.'

And no, Bernie Simmonds didn't remember me from that first assembly of heathen Catholics and Jews. He didn't even remember the pear. Jeananne's boyfriend at the time was the extremely intelligent and thoughtful *Guardian* journalist, Alan Ruisbridger. Next morning I met one of her housemates, another journalist, Christopher Hitchens, whose by-line I had often seen in *The New Statesman*. The following night (Jeananne having gone to bed) Alan, Christopher, Bernie and I talked for hours over Bernie's whiskey. The two journalists were about my age, but their careers were inexorably rising. Bernie, furthermore, a dedicated libertarian whose professional energies were perhaps intensified by an unhappily repressed homosexuality, was already one of the great rising legal eminences of London. To be sure, Christopher, radiant as uranium, was clearly the charismatic star at that table of four men, but intellectually, I was not hugely inferior to my companions. Yet I sensed three illustrious careers were taking off moonwards, while I was the landbound spectator, shielding my envious eyes against the white light of their booster flames. I knew I had to make something more of my life, and to do that, I had to leave Belfast and return to Dublin. And in due course, I did.

I already had one main project in mind when I made that move, which was to restore to the people of Ireland a memory of the forgotten Irish dead of the Great War. The seeds of this had been sown during the conversations with my father in my childhood, which had then been watered by the discovery of the magazine in the locker at Ratcliffe. So when I resumed my life as a journalist in Dublin, I began to write about the roughly 300,000 Irishmen who had served with the British armed forces in 1914–18 and who had since been completely forgotten, their deeds consciously obliterated by the political forces of the new state that had emerged after that time. And I do mean, completely forgotten, as if they had never existed.

By the early 1980s I had become an established columnist with *The Irish Times*, and during this time, in the context of my Great War columns, I wrote of my recent and entirely accidental discovery that in 1856 a relative (a Teevan of my mother's family) had survived the famously suicidal Charge of the Light Brigade of the Crimean War.

A COUPLE of days later, I got a phone call. The voice was old and hesitant, but it had an edge to it: a slight sneer, even.

'Is that Kevin Myers?'

'Yes, it is.'

'You're always going on about the Irish in the Great War,' said the voice. 'Now you're boasting about what this ancestor of yours did in the Crimean War. Why don't you tell them about your father?'

'My father? What about my father?'

'Your father was the finest soldier I ever served with.'

Dad, a soldier? A brief pause for a smile. 'No, I'm afraid you're mistaken there,' I replied. 'You must be talking about another Myers.'

'Is your father Willie Myers?'

'He was. He's dead now.'

'God rest his soul, I thought he might be. He'd have been getting on if he were still alive. Like myself. To be sure, now ... was he the son of Jack Myers of the Dublin Fire Brigade?'

A forgivable mistake. (To remind you: my great-uncle Jack, then a lieutenant in the Dublin Fire Brigade, along with his sister

Margaret, had raised his nephew Willie, my father, and Dad's two sisters, Pat and Nellie, while Jack's brother William, the father of the three children, worked down the country as a policeman.)

'No, not the son,' I replied. 'His nephew. But Jack Myers raised him.'

'We're talking about the same Willie Myers, so. I knew him when he was a young fella. And this Teevan fellow … he was on your mother's side?'

'He was. My mother's name is Teevan.'

'An unusual name. There was a Judge Teevan.'

'My uncle.'

'Ah, so Willie Myers married well. I could tell by the cut of him he would. Lookit, do you think we could ever meet?'

That evening, I walked into Bowes' pub across the road. A wizened old fellow raised a curt hand in greeting as he saw me.

'Dan Foley,' he said. 'What are you having?' We each had a coffee.

'You were saying about my father,' I said after some polite small talk.

'The finest soldier I ever met,' he replied in a very decisive voice.

'But my father wasn't a soldier.'

'He most certainly was. He was in F Company, 2nd Battalion, Dublin Brigade, IRA, with me.'

'The IRA? I don't think so.'

'Oh yes he was. And a very keen soldier, too. Maybe he didn't talk about the past very much.'

Well, of course, he did: about the Royal Dublin Fusiliers in Flanders, and Willie Doyle, and the blood of the Irish soldiers filling the bay of Sed-el-Bahr in Gallipoli, all in the British service. He taught me to sing 'British Grenadiers', and had also told me how he hated the IRA – but I didn't say that to Dan Foley.

'So when were you and Dad in the IRA together?'

'War of Independence, 1919–21. We did our bit. Me and him, and Charlie Dalton. Your father's best friend.'

The name Charlie Dalton was only slightly familiar to me, and I admitted as much to Dan Foley.

'The way of true heroes. They're easily forgotten. Charlie Dalton was a member of The Squad. You know what I mean by The Squad?' I did, vaguely. It was an assassination unit set up by Michael Collins, which he used in the ferocious murder campaign that was a key part of the IRA's War of Independence.

'Are you saying that my father was one of The Squad?' I asked, astonished. If this was a lie, it was a very big one.

'One thing at a time,' he laughed, apparently pleased at my discomfiture. 'One thing at a time. You're jumping ahead of the game here. Your father was impetuous like that too. I read your stuff. You're very pro-British. Being true to the land of your birth, I suppose.'

'Being anti-IRA isn't being pro-British.'

'It is where I come from,' he said quietly. 'The IRA is just continuing the holy struggle that I fought in long ago here in Dublin. I go to all the IRA funerals in Belfast, even still.' He finished his coffee. 'I've enjoyed talking to you. You have your father's face, I see. The same eyes. We must meet again. I'll telephone you.'

'How can I contact you?'

'You can't.' And so saying, this elderly man slipped into the Dublin night.

I didn't hear from him for a couple of weeks. He rang one afternoon, and we again arranged to meet in Bowes' pub. This time I was there before him, and he laughed. 'One-upmanship, I see, getting in nice and early. Mick Collins always respected punctuality. He said, "We'll teach the fucking British that an Irishman can read a clock as well they can."'

His face had a mirthless smile on it. 'I was thinking,' he said, as he sipped his coffee. 'I can tell you a lot about your father's time with me and Charlie Dalton in the IRA. The thing is … do you want to know it all? You being so pro-British and so on.' He laughed that bitter little laugh again.

'I'll hear whatever you have to tell me. I'm here, aren't I?'

'You are, you are. I'm just giving you a chance to reflect. Lookit. Here's a number you can get me at … leave a message if I'm out.' He handed me a piece of paper with just a number on it.

'No name,' I observed.

'Old habits die hard.'

'Very old habits,' I joked.

He looked at me coldly. 'They started long ago. But the war goes on. You give me a ring when you've thought about this a bit more. Ask for Dan. Just Dan.'

I thought about this matter very closely and did some research on Charlie Dalton. This was easy: a lot of the stuff was on file and microfilm in the *Irish Times* library. The IRA had made a killer of Dalton when he was just sixteen, during its campaign against 'G Division' of the Dublin Metropolitan Police from 1919 onwards. History, I now know, has bestowed a wholly undeserved glamour on these deeds. The victims were not ruthless, pro-British zealots, but mostly ordinary Irish Catholic countrymen who, like my grandfather, joined the police before the violence of 1916 had changed the political scene for ever. They were not traitors in any useful sense of the word, just minor government functionaries. Yet one by one, they were nonetheless murdered.

Worse still was to come. Just before breakfast one Sunday morning in November 1920, scores of IRA men were involved in the attempted mass murder of some twenty-four sleeping, half-naked men in their bedrooms across Dublin. Twelve of the attempts were successful. Some of the victims were relatively minor British agents, many were not. Men were slain before their screaming wives: one pregnant wife lost her child within days of becoming a widow. That afternoon, British forces completed another glorious day for Ireland with the slaughter of over a dozen spectators at a football match in Dublin. In all, thirty-five people were killed on what is rightly known as Bloody Sunday.

Could Dad really have been associated with the IRA butchery that had begun this terrible day? Not merely had he always been anti-IRA, but his father – my grandfather – had been an RIC policeman, and Uncle Jack, who had raised him, was a loyal servant of the crown. I rang my mother. She knew nothing whatsoever about Dan Foley's story about Dad having been in the IRA. She and Dad had met some fourteen years after these terrible events, and he had never spoken to her about that time. 'Go and see Uncle Martin,' she urged.

Martin Coffey, now a widower after the death of Dad's sister Pat, was a genial man of the utmost integrity who, I knew, had some tenuous links to the IRA in the olden days. I went to his home in Frankfort Avenue. His next-door neighbour was a kindly old Protestant woman named Violett – two t's, she insisted when she told me her name – who had, during earlier visits, told me that she had spent her life minding her brother Reggie. He had been gassed and crippled while serving with the British army in the Great War, in which she had also lost her fiancé. 'Pardon me for being so rude,' she once told me, 'but I could never marry after that. My bowels have never been right since the day the telegram arrived.' (A slightly fuller description of this encounter is in my book, *Ireland's Great War*.)

I suppose Martin and she kept their very distinct stories apart, even as I heard them both, but separately. For that has been the Irish way throughout the twentieth century, myths co-existing while silently contradicting, and so surviving. On this occasion, Martin sat beside the fireplace, as he always did, his feet up on the table, tamping his pipe while he listened to my story about Dan Foley.

He thought for a while before replying. 'Your father was a good man. He was, as this Dan Foley has told you, in the IRA. He swore me to secrecy and I've never told anyone, not even your aunt Pat. But I cannot tell a lie. You asked me a direct question. I'd never have told you if you hadn't.'

'And Charlie Dalton?'

He stopped talking for a while. 'He and your father were good friends. But look … what does this Dan Foley fellow want? Why's he doing this?'

I didn't know, of course.

Martin sniffed thoughtfully. 'Listen. Terrible things happened at that time. Things that shouldn't have happened, but they did. Just ask yourself this question. You've told me some of the stuff you've been through up North. Do you really want to hear about your father might have become involved in? Is that what you want?'

I didn't say anything.

'There was a reason why your father swore me to silence. You don't know what it was. But I do. And I can tell you now that I'll never tell you what that reason was. As for this Dan Foley fellow, it's up to you whether or not you listen to him.'

Martin's manner was kind but firm. I realized as I left that something special had always bound Martin and Dad. Those times standing mute on Greystones beach, gazing at dark, restless seas. There was a point of access to their secrets, and it lay on that piece of paper in my pocket. Over the coming days and weeks, I occasionally looked at it. But I never contacted Dan Foley, just as he never again contacted me, and so I never heard his account of what Dad had done as an IRA man, and nor did dear Martin ever tell me another thing before he too passed on.

AND IT ALL might have rested there. But as happenstance has repeatedly waved a magnet over the compass of my life, so it intervened again. Quite independently of this account, years after Foley contacted me, I was searching in an online newspaper archive for an IRA insurgent with the unusual name of Holohan. In the moments of the 1916 Rising in Dublin, this Holohan had cold-bloodedly shot dead an unarmed Irish boy called Playfair, and I was doing a name search to see what had become of Holohan. But instead, my search accidentally found a victim named Holohan, some six years after the Rising, in the autumn of 1922.

The previous spring, the newly independent Irish Free State had come into existence, and Dad's best friend, Charlie Dalton, with a half-dozen unarmed dead men to his name, had been commissioned as major into the new Free State Army, his skill as an assassin being his only apparent qualification for officer rank. Shortly afterwards the new State collapsed into a civil war that even now defies rational understanding: only the logic of Cain, and perhaps of the Charlie Daltons of this world, can explain it.

In September 1922 the now pro-government Commandant Charles Dalton, in the new Irish army uniform, arrested three teenage boys who were distributing anti-government leaflets in the north Dublin suburb of Drumcondra. They were Edwin Hughes (seventeen), Joseph Rogers (sixteen) and the barium in this historical meal, Brendan Holohan (sixteen). That night, Commandant Dalton (twenty) drove the three youngsters to a hamlet called The Red Cow, just outside Dublin, where the next morning, the lads' dead bodies were found, riddled with bullets. Some days later, an inquest into the killings was opened and then adjourned, and never reinstated. Commandant Dalton had already been arrested and charged with the murders, but as the Civil War raged, the charges were quietly dropped and then forgotten, and he returned to his duties as an army officer.

No history book has ever referred to these murders, just as Irish history books have systematically ignored so much of what is unpalatable and murderous about the IRA campaign that preceded and essentially authorized them. However, this was no personal concern of mine, for both Dan Foley and Martin had assured me that Dad was not involved in the Civil War. He was therefore not associated with these murders. But he had been a close friend and comrade of the man who committed them. So, having made the discovery of Dalton's triple murder, long since forgotten by history, I wrote a column about it. I was soon afterwards contacted by a rather surprised member of the Dalton family. The Daltons had never heard about the Red Cow killings. Could we meet?

We did, and I was told the outline history of Charlie Dalton's life. Unlike Dad, Charles Dalton had done well out of his days in the IRA. After leaving the Irish army Dalton went on to become a director of the first great fraud of the new Irish state, the Irish Hospital Sweeps, which raised vast fortunes in Britain and the US, supposedly for Irish medical care, though in reality huge chunks went into the pockets of the former gunmen who were running it, such as its founder, Joe McGrath. And some also went into the pockets of his assistant, Charlie Dalton, who soon settled in salubrious Morehampton Road – the very epicentre of the Bloody Sunday butchery of 1920. The wages of sin, it seems, is not death, but a house in the most fashionable area of Dublin, amid the scenes of one's past glories. Charlie lived in number 86. Two of those terrible murders had been done in numbers 47 and 117.

And so all turned out well with Charlie Dalton, seasoned killer? Not quite. For actually, Dalton had spent the last years of his life in a mental hospital, a broken alcoholic, a sobbing ruin who when he was not weeping was wailing. Indeed, if anything, his dementia seemed by a very wide margin to exceed the fate that Dad had endured.

I checked with the Bureau of Military Archives, which had recorded an interview with Charles Dalton about his glorious fight for Irish freedom. Needless to say, the archive had nothing about the Red Cow triple murders. In his account, Dalton named his primary IRA active service unit as The Squad, but he listed his original unit as F Company, 2nd Battalion, Dublin Brigade, IRA – the same company in which Dan Foley told me that he and Dad had served.

Dalton also reported that whenever The Squad's order book for assassinations was too full, it routinely farmed out its killings to one particular IRA unit: F Company, 2nd Battalion, Dublin IRA. These hits included many on that butcher's dawn of Bloody

Sunday, as well as many Irish civilians that were merely suspected of being enemies of the IRA. Such slayings became increasingly commonplace in the early summer of 1921. Was my father involved in such deeds? I do not know. But I do know that in my lifetime he deeply and passionately hated the IRA and its deeds. I also know that the state, which came into existence as a result of the IRA terrorist campaign, in which had he served, had then robbed him of his job, so forcing him into exile.

In that exile, he came to support the last vestiges of the empire he had once opposed by force of arms. He bade us particularly to respect old Mr Campbell, the Irish ex-policeman who had been forced into earlier exile by the new Irish State because he had served the British, against the IRA and therefore, in effect, against my father. Now, these two former enemies had become mutually respectful neighbours in their common exile. Finally, like his friend and fellow gunman Charlie Dalton, my father was to spend the final years of his life a broken man.

Furthermore, it was only while I was working on this account that I came to realize that Dad's breakdown had actually coincided with the start of yet another IRA terrorist campaign in Northern Ireland. It was this that had prompted his outburst against the IRA. Had the renewal of yet another such meaningless war also prompted insupportable memories of the deeds he had done? I simply do not know.

So how many other men who had followed Michael Collins' inspiration, and had taken the lives of their fellow Irishmen, were themselves broken in their later years, as they looked back to the days of their youth and the people they had slain? How many lives had been ruined by such killings – initially and primarily of course, those of their victims, and their victims' families, but far later, of their perpetrators also, and their families also?

My father was not bound for medicine when he was drawn to the ranks of the IRA and thereby to murder. Medicine only came after the truce in 1921. Why did he join the IRA? Was saving life his later compensation for lives that he had helped to take? Did he spend the rest of his days making recompense for the deeds of his youth? All these questions, yet answers are there none, not least because those with the most serious implications are also the most hypothetical.

Not all killers ended up like Dad and Charlie Dalton. One leader of a Bloody Sunday murder squad was a lad called Seán Lemass, who went on to become the main fixer of the Irish government in the 1940s. It was he who got all the vital government jobs for the boys during the period when my father's job was given to a relative of a party placeman. Which was perhaps why Dad had cursed Lemass after his discovery of Uncle Jack's name in *Ulysses*.

And there could well be a subtext to this: for Dad had lost his job in a transport company that was being nationalized soon after the appearance of a death notice in *The Irish Times* for Captain Kevin Teevan, RAMC, with Dad's address attached. Might the loss of his job have been punishment upon Dad for having such pro-British links? Certainly, after the war, Fianna Fáil – the party that had effectively exiled Dad – put a permanent bar on government jobs or welfare for all Irish army soldiers who had deserted to serve the Allied cause.

Dad joined the IRA when he was not much older than I was at Ratcliffe, where my intemperate righteousness brought ruin to five largely decent lads. And had I not later become a student radical, than which there is barely anything more righteously vapid in this world? A toxic thing, this righteousness, for it authorizes the boundless ecstasies of the lynch mob, it sandstones the eager steel of the guillotine, and it steadies the hand of the gunman in the shadows. So what terrible things might I have done, had I been an ardent youngster in the violent Dublin of my father's youth? For my face is my father's face, my build is my father's build, and even my sorry ways are pitifully his. Within our two separate ribcages, some half a century apart, a time-travelling anatomist might find the same, reckless organ: a single headstrong heart.